AMBROSE BIERCE TAKES ON THE RA
ILROAD   THE JOURNALIST AS MUC
KRAKER AND CYNIC

LINDLEY, DANIEL   1956-

Ambrose Bierce Takes on the Railroad

Ambrose Bierce Takes on the Railroad

The Journalist as Muckraker and Cynic

Daniel Lindley

Westport, Connecticut
London

Library of Congress Cataloging-in-Publication Data

Lindley, Daniel
    Ambrose Bierce takes on the railroad : the journalist as muckraker
and cynic / Daniel Lindley.
      p.   cm.
   Includes bibliographical references and index.
   ISBN 0–275–96696–8 (alk. paper)
   1. Bierce, Ambrose, 1842–1914?—Knowledge—Journalism.
  2. Railroads—Political aspects—California—History.
  3. Journalism—California—San Francisco—History. 4. Authors,
American—19th century—Biography. 5. Journalists—United States—
Biography. I. Title.
PS1097.Z5L56   1999
813′.4—dc21   99–21193

British Library Cataloguing in Publication Data is available.

Library of Congress Catalog Card Number: 99–21193
ISBN: 0–275–96696–8

First published in 1999

Praeger Publishers, 88 Post Road West, Westport, CT 06881
An imprint of Greenwood Publishing Group, Inc.
www.praeger.com

Printed in the United States of America

The paper used in this book complies with the
Permanent Paper Standard issued by the National
Information Standards Organization (Z39.48–1984).

10 9 8 7 6 5 4 3 2 1

In memory of my father,
Francis Vinton Lindley

Contents

A photo essay follows Chapter 5.

1

Introduction

Ambrose Bierce, when he is remembered at all, is recalled usually for his short, grizzly pieces of fiction, or perhaps for the hydrochloric set of aphorisms he published in *The Devil's Dictionary*. Seldom is he associated with journalism, although he spent nearly his entire working life writing for one newspaper or another. Nearly all his published writing, in fact, may be considered journalism in a sense, since practically all of it, including fiction, articles, columns, aphorisms, parodies, commentary, and other work, originally appeared in newspapers or magazines.

Largely forgotten as a journalist, Bierce is also an unlikely muckraker at first glance. Muckrakers commonly are associated with sober and purposeful if perhaps earnest and even naive efforts at reform. Bierce responded to the world with a cosmic cackle. His fiery, coruscating, slashing prose did not evoke the plodding reformer. He could tear down but could not build, and did not want to.

That Bierce was a muckraker, albeit an unlikely one not only in style but in time and place, is the argument of this work. Part of its task will be to define muckraking, perhaps not as easy a chore as it seems. Like geographic boundaries, definitions can be arbitrary and can shift over time. But a definition of the salient traits of the muckrakers who followed Bierce's most active period in journalism by only a decade helps place him in that tradition.

Such a definition requires a review of the background of the muckrakers as well as of the style and method of their journalism. It also entails an evaluation of the impact and overall success of the genre.

Comparing and contrasting the art and craft of the muckrakers with Bierce and his journalistic jihad against Collis P. Huntington and the Central Pacific Railroad is not an attempt to pigeonhole Bierce as a muckraker. He excelled at many different types of writing (and failed miserably at a few). Certainly, his muckraking campaign amounted to only one small though important part of his life.

A closer examination of Bierce in the unlikely role of muckraker will shed light not only on Bierce's career but on the muckraker's calling as well. Perhaps, by extension, such a comparison might even illumine the efforts of later generations of muckrakers—not only of the "literature of exposure's" possibilities, but of its inherent limitations as well.

In many ways, Bierce was a muckraker, though not 100 percent true to type. But Bierce did not fit any mold. Few if any of the "real" muckrakers were 100 percent sure of their cause. Neither does it appear that he was a major influence on the muckrakers themselves. His influence on future journalists, such as it was, appears to have run quite to the contrary. One can see traces of Bierce, for instance, in the writings of H. L. Mencken, who most decidedly was not a muckraker.

Bierce commonly used irony in both his nonfiction and his fiction, and his own life was not without its twists, many of them cruel. Perhaps he savored his own reverses less than the ones he recorded in his stories. In any event, by the time the muckraking era as defined by most historians rolled around shortly after the start of the twentieth century, he surely must have felt that it had passed him by. He had come to see in his own life the inherent limits of that brand of journalism and to revile the less-than-pure motives of the publishers, editors, and writers who were eager to accommodate a changing marketplace of ideas. He was disillusioned and withdrawn from the world, bitter, cynical, old, and complaining. After he finished assembling his collected works— surely a true ending for a man who had made his living nearly all his life by writing—there was little left to do but disappear without a trace, leaving the year and place of his death a permanent question mark in encyclopedia entries. Naturally, his earlier involvement in muckraking did not cause all of the bitterness and pain of his last years. But certainly his own limited success and ambivalent experience with the genre must have colored his thought.

Bierce always insisted that each word bore only one real and true meaning (a point upon which he harped most insistently in *Write It Right*, a kind of early Strunk and White writer's handbook). That rigid approach to the English language may help explain the strength, and the weakness, that various readers have found in his writing: the crystalline clarity that many critics have praised, and the aridity and sterility that many have denigrated.

Perhaps he would have appreciated a crucial distinction that helps explain a misconception about his life and work. It lies in the double meaning of the word "cynic." He was indeed a cynic, which would appear to disqualify him from being classified as a muckraker. How can one be a reformer and a cynic at the same time? The answer may lie in the word's multiple meanings. Until the last few years of his known existence, Bierce was not a cynic, at least in the way the word is commonly defined, as a selfish, unprincipled person in dishonest pursuit of worldly goods—in Oscar Wilde's definition, "a man who knows the price of everything and the value of nothing." Collis P. Huntington, Bierce's railroad adversary, would be a far superior exemplar of that definition.

Bierce was a Cynic in the classical sense. This entailed a world-weary view that proposed that life was a selfish round of vanity heaped upon vanity. But such Cynicism did not recommend selfishness to its adherents, nor did it even propose embittered retreat as necessarily the proper reaction to the world's fundamental meanness and quotidian swindling. Rather, it urged a selfless offensive against all falsehood, deceit, and vanity, albeit with the foregone conclusion that all such attacks ultimately would be in vain. The Stoics and other classical writers Bierce studied as a young man struck some resonant chord within. They were not too different, in disdainful view of human nature and in impossible ideals, from Bierce's own Puritan antecedents.

Few men embrace anything completely, and certainly so complex a man as Bierce probably had reservations about his own path, insofar as he could choose it. He had left his own background far behind. He quit all communication with his parents and nearly all his siblings after leaving home when he was young. In attempting to escape the shackles of midwestern protestantism and its residue of New England Puritanism, he wound up combining them with Stoicism and Cynicism, all curiously transplanted in the fertile soil of California. He reacted to the failed dreams of the old midwestern frontier by making a new stand farther west, just as earlier Bierces had headed west to Ohio from Connecticut. His later days and style of journalism plainly reflected his early days.

At the same time, Huntington and his railroad represented new but not better times. They were to become for Bierce another in a series of disillusions, not only for Bierce but for the nation. In opening up and settling the West, they not only helped close the frontier, Americans' age-old escape valve, but helped change and corrupt the character of the nation and the way its business was carried on.

The railroad sometimes unwittingly changed newspapers while it consciously altered the landscape and commerce. In part, its ultimate defeat—after nearly half a century of dominating California politics— can be attributed to the rise of yellow journalism and muckraking, which it had helped create by bringing about a national market through the transportation of goods. This broader, more dynamic market had aided a general transition from a subsidized party press to a modern system built on circulation and advertising.

But the railroad meanwhile continued to subsidize papers as if they were still members of an old-fashioned party press, although it did so on a far grander and more corrupt scale and, in Solomonic manner, disbursed funds to both parties. The strategy succeeded for a long time. Railroad officials had bought much of the goodwill of the California press. Publishers who had dared oppose the railroad had simply been flattened by its enormous power. Eventually, men like Hearst came along who had the money, brains, and courage not only to challenge it, but to understand the circulation benefits possible from making the attack. Although Bierce despised the railroad men, Hearst's counterattack ultimately violated Bierce's rather aristocratic ideals.

The railroad's background and Bierce's require a little explanation. This is as much a story of men as of institutions, and an effort will be made to fill in some of the details of the personal struggles involved. Although no attempt will be made at psychobiography or psychohistory, one can't help but notice the uneasy relationship of many of the main characters with their patrimony: a tale of men as interested, perhaps, in remaking themselves as in remaking the world. Among them was Grove Johnson, a politician who spent his career groveling before the railroad; his son Hiram Johnson, who eventually became Progressive governor of California by running on a platform seeking to control the railroad; Collis P. Huntington, rapacious millionaire, the rough and poor son of a tinker; William R. Hearst, at least for a time a self-styled "man of the people," son of Senator George Hearst, who had struggled up to riches and political power from obscure beginnings; and Ambrose, son of Marcus Aurelius, but far different from the Roman emperor who was his namesake.

Bierce and His Biographers

THE PRESS AND THE RAILROAD

On a May day in 1869, Leland Stanford stood poised above a railroad track in Promontory, Utah, wielding a silver hammer that was to drive the final spike connecting the rails of the nation's first transcontinental railroad. For more than six years, the Central Pacific Railroad had inched eastward from Sacramento over the Sierra Nevada range and across the desert, while the Union Pacific had made more rapid progress westward across the plains.

As the rails came near their meeting point, the predominantly Chinese crews of the Central Pacific and the mainly Irish crews of the Union Pacific had raced, more for the millions of dollars in federal subsidies each mile of track meant for their employers than for the sake of national pride. So hasty were they, in fact, that they overshot their mark, and the men stubbornly continued laying tracks in parallel. Perhaps the work would have gone on without end had not a commission convened and declared Promontory the official junction.

The former governor of and future senator from California raised the silver hammer, swung, and missed the spike that was to unite the nation. A telegrapher stationed nearby ignored Stanford's ineptness, however, and obligingly if dishonestly signaled the nation that the final link had been made. As the news arrived over the wires, a magnetic ball dropped from a pole above the Capitol dome at Washington, D.C., bells began to peal in San Francisco, and similar demonstrations of rejoicing began to take place across the land.

The report, not exactly truthful, set the theme for the relationship between the Central Pacific, of which Stanford was a principal, and the nation's press, especially California's newspapers, for the next forty years. The Central Pacific in its western stronghold was to become more powerful than local and state governments, according to many contemporary and historical accounts. Through the distribution of subsidies as well as other favors, it controlled a host of newspapers as well as politicians. In effect, newspaper editors mimicked the Utah telegrapher who had ignored Stanford's wild swing of the hammer. They spread only good news about the railroad, or at least downplayed or ignored the bad.

At the height of its power, the railroad controlled politics and newspapers in ten western states and territories.[1] Its influence, according to one writer, made Boss Tweed's brazenly corrupt political operation in New York seem "localized and trifling" in comparison.[2] Though nominally Republican in its political affiliation—Stanford, during his tenure as California's first Republican governor, had lobbied for federal approval of the railroad even though he stood to benefit financially from the nascent enterprise—the railroad did not quibble over mere party politics, and controlled some Democratic politicians as well. It cast its influence, mainly through the distribution of free passes and through outright bribes, to all levels of political and judicial office, and to newspapers from the smallest rural weeklies to the biggest urban dailies.[3]

This is, at least, the way the scene has been painted by many contemporaries and by most historians. There have been a few dissenters but usually their motives have been suspect. Cerinda W. Evans, for instance, in her biography of the Central Pacific's guiding light, Collis P. Huntington, maintains that Huntington and his railroad have been the victims of scurrilous and defamatory attack. The Mariners' Museum, a beneficiary of a Huntington family legacy, was the publisher of her book, however. Its frontispiece contains an epigraph that is a typical Huntington homily, one of many that he fed the press during his long and successful career and which seemed to justify the social and financial heights he had scaled: "Success in life only means honesty of purpose and intelligent economy."[4]

BIERCE AND THE "OCTOPUS"

Although the press has been painted as meek in reacting to Huntington's larcenies, historians usually have singled out one journalist for consistently tangling with the railroad octopus, as it had come to be known long before Frank Norris published his novel of the same name in 1901. That railroad adversary, Ambrose Bierce, is better known today for his mysterious disappearance in Mexico, a legend carried on in Hollywood fables like *The Old Gringo*.

In 1869, when Stanford and his fellow dignitaries were assembling in Promontory, Bierce had been in California for a little more than two years. Having recently assumed editorship of the *San Francisco News-Letter* after a few years of eking out a living at the U.S. Sub-Treasury office and as a freelance writer, he was rising in public stature. In 1872, he left for England, where he stayed for three years, sharpening his skills writing for English journals. He returned to California in 1875 (unwillingly and at the behest of his wife, Mary Ellen "Mollie" Day Bierce, who was adding a daughter, Helen, to the two sons, Day and Leigh, she had already borne him). There he secured his reputation for wielding one of the most caustic pens in the West. He was, by stages over the next three decades, an editor and writer for two San Francisco magazines, the *Argonaut* and the *Wasp*, and, beginning in 1887, a columnist for William Randolph Hearst's *San Francisco Examiner*. Later he also wrote for Hearst's *New York Journal* and *Cosmopolitan*.

Bierce often has been cited as a voice crying out in the western wilderness against the rapacity of the railroad, but the reasons for his opposition, the manner of his methods, and the extent of his success have been variously interpreted. Many of his biographers have concentrated on his crusade, undertaken at the order of his boss, William Randolph Hearst, against the Pacific Refunding Bill. The funding bill, as it was more commonly known, arose from a scheme pushed by railroad officials in the 1890s to avoid or, alternatively, reduce and extend repayment of the millions of dollars of loans the federal government had provided to build the railroad. These bonds were shortly to come due.

Hearst sent Bierce to Washington in 1896 to cover congressional debate over the funding bill, and some writers have concentrated on this brief trip to the exclusion of all else, as if Bierce's concern with the railroad began and ended with that one piece of legislation. Not only have most such accounts focused on the funding bill battle, but they usually have sketched Bierce's struggle against the bill as an unparalleled success.

Writers have disagreed about Bierce's reasons for making the fight. They have attempted to explain his hatred of the railroad in a number of ways, giving as his reasons a defiantly moral attitude focused on the dishonesty of the railroad's owners, or a concern for the victims of the railroad's high rates and strongarm political tactics, or even an inbred resistance to authority resulting from an unhappy childhood. A onetime friend of Bierce traced his antipathy to a need for vengeance, claiming he was angry because the railroad had not granted him a public relations job when he was a young man in California.

Such accounts often have been based on previous ones, and merely serve to repeat rather than illuminate. Ernest Jerome Hopkins has done the most nearly complete job of reviewing Bierce's fight against the Central Pacific.[5] His project on Bierce and the "Rail-Rogues" reprints many, but not all, of Bierce's San Francisco Examiner articles on the funding bill debate, but includes only a smattering of Bierce's anti-railroad articles before then.

Hopkins's analysis is scant and not particularly revelatory. It focuses on the funding bill and skims over Bierce's earlier work. Hopkins closely follows the judgments of two writers who were contemporaries of Bierce: Fremont Older, a San Francisco newspaper reporter and editor, and Charles Edward Russell, a muckraker who wrote a series for Hampton's Magazine in 1910 exposing the misdeeds not only of the Southern Pacific, which became the Central Pacific's parent company, but also of many of the nation's other railroads.[6]

Hopkins quotes Russell's glowing characterization of Bierce's work against the funding bill: "This may be held to be as wonderful a victory as ever was achieved by one man's pen, and, also, one of the most remarkable tributes to the power of persistent publicity."[7] He goes on to paraphrase Russell's conclusion, which suggests that the victory was Pyrrhic. Although the railroad did finally agree to pay its government debts, it managed to do so with little or no discomfort to its owners by issuing new stock and debt and by saddling the public with higher freight rates to cover the payments. Russell concluded that the public ended up paying about $70 million more by this arrangement than it would have had the debt simply been forgiven.[8]

Inspired by Horace Greeley's example, Older burned to become a newspaper reporter and had come to California from the Midwest when he was sixteen years old. He succeeded in landing newspaper jobs in Sacramento and eventually in San Francisco, where he developed an intimate personal and business acquaintance with the Octopus. Later, brooding much on its tight embrace, he wrote substantially the same conclusion as Russell, crediting Bierce with a magnificent funding bill victory but noting that the sale of new railroad securities and an increase in rates had hollowed that triumph.

Older had a good vantage point: not only was he in a position to watch the railroad's public machinations from his post as editor of the *San Francisco Bulletin*, but he also enjoyed personal knowledge of its private ways because the *Bulletin* happened to be on the railroad's payroll. In the years after Bierce's victory, he declared, the railroad's power did not diminish but rather "became more absolute and more insolent."[9]

In his "Rail-Rogue" study, Hopkins concedes that the funding bill fight was not a complete triumph for Bierce, but that it was in any event a grand if limited advance. In another work, however, he seems to have concluded that Bierce's wit cut a far wider swath. He suggests that "since the Progressive Party, the Bull Moose campaign, the presidency of Woodrow Wilson, and the Franklin Delano Roosevelt campaign stemmed in sequence from the breaking of the 'Rail-Rogues' power in California and the West, it is apparent that the combination of Hearst's aggressiveness with Bierce's satire played a not inconsiderable part in history."[10] The implication is plain, even if built on sweeping assumption and tautology: that Bierce's attacks did in the railroad, that the railroad's downfall ushered in the Progressive and later "liberal" eras, and that Bierce was not only a forerunner of the Progressives but indeed a catalyst of an entire era because he had happened to come before them and to attack the railroad.

If Hopkins's logic sometimes is tenuous, his scope is at least broad. He is one of the few who traces Bierce's antagonism to the railroad before 1896, although his investigations are sporadic. Despite his sketchy presentation of earlier material, he does make an effort to explain the source of Bierce's ferocious hatred of the railroad, tracing its roots to the Mussel Slough massacre of 1880, in which railroad thugs and government lawmen killed a handful of protesting farmers in the San Joaquin Valley. The incident helped turn the public against the railroad, according to Hopkins, and when Bierce joined the *Wasp* in 1881, he faced a dilemma: whether to attack the railroad, for whose "tyranny" he had a "natural hatred," or oppose the farmers, whose actions were illegal.

He could have sided with the farmers or, like the railroad-subsidized press, maintained silence. He compromised, according to Hopkins, and chose "to step in with both feet—against both sides, the railroad primarily." Overall, in the Hopkins view, Bierce's effort against the railroad was a dramatic success: "Satire, evidently, had the power to start a new trend where oppressive and violent means had failed. Moderns take note."[11]

In general, thought on Bierce's attacks on the railroad has been divided in three parts. A few consider him a muckraker or at least a progenitor of the breed. Like Hopkins and Older, many others praise his newspaper and magazine campaign (and often overrate its overall impact) but make little or no attempt to relate it to muckraking. Three attack Bierce as a charlatan. Practically all, whether admiring or critical, describe his work as successful.

A biographer and two dissertationists who have provided some of the best insights into Bierce's journalism put him in the muckraking camp without really saying much about muckraking. Carey McWilliams, long-time editor of the *Nation* and the most insightful, thorough, and sympathetic of Bierce's biographers, describes the funding bill fight as epochal:

Not only was the defeat of the railroad a great achievement in itself, but the consequences of the victory can scarcely be overestimated. It marked the doom of Southern Pacific dominance in California. The tide had turned and it did not cease rolling on to victory until Hiram Johnson had been elected Governor.[12]

In reviewing Bierce's funding bill articles, McWilliams concludes that Bierce reined in his satire—abandoning the "unmodulated journalism" of his early days"[13]—and that he became a forerunner of the muckrakers, with one important difference:

Long before his colleagues, David Graham Phillips and Alfred Henry Lewis, started their muckraking journalism, Mr. Bierce had fought and won a most decisive victory over one of the worst monopolies that ever disgraced this country. But he had drawn no hasty inferences, and once the fight was over, it was for him a closed chapter. Would that there had been other journalists as sensible![14]

Lawrence I. Berkove suggests that the fight over the funding bill brought Bierce "journalistic fame" and that he played "an important role" in defeating it.[15] In the face of "so powerful and well-financed a lobby," he reports, "by dint of extraordinary investigative reporting and forceful writing, Bierce brought about the defeat of the bill. Then, years later, when the muckrakers began their exposés of big business, Bierce's example guided them."[16]

Bierce's barrage against the funding bill did indeed qualify him as a muckraker, Janet M. Francendese avers, noting that the articles depart from the normal epigrammatic style of his columns and that they are introduced with "copious" headlines.[17] She identifies a principle central to Bierce's journalism—his tactic of ridiculing particular persons in an effort to attack a more general and abstract but particular vice—and finds that it worked in this case. Bierce's "fierce pursuit of the 'Rail-Rogues' not only defeated the funding bill, but also dealt a mortal blow to Collis Huntington's political influence in California."[18]

Many writers refrain from placing Bierce in the muckraking tradition. Some argue against it. One biographer, Richard O'Connor, concludes that even though Bierce realized he owed part of his success to Hearst's political aspirations, "in the role of St. George, Bierce performed with a gusto—and an instinct for his opponent's jugular—that resulted, in great part, in a surprising defeat for one of the robber baron generation which had never been really challenged since the Civil War."[19] In O'Connor's view, however, the term "muckraker," at least as applied to Bierce, is "inexact." Although muckrakers expose "evil" conditions, Bierce viewed the practice with "distaste" and "was not so much the investigative reporter in his crusade against the Southern Pacific as a satirist, gadfly and angry prophet."[20]

Bierce "deservedly [won] national renown for uncovering the most diabolical transportation plot that, until then, had been revealed in the United States," declares Walter Neale, one of Bierce's publishers and biographers. But if Bierce were a muckraker, or even an investigative journalist, he was an unwilling one, according to Neale. Bierce even resisted Hearst's efforts to get him to conduct interviews, considering such journalistic methods beneath his station. Even so, he "used to some degree the methods of journalism that he professed to abhor, cursing his employer all the while."[21]

Richard Saunders and Roy Morris, Jr. have little to say about Bierce as muckraker, although they correctly trace the beginning of his railroad attacks to the anti-railroad *Wasp*. Saunders depicts Bierce as "a long-time opponent of these greedy and unbelievably ruthless railroad tycoons who all but owned California after the financial collapse of the Seventies"[22] and claims that Bierce's antipathy began after the massacre of railroad opponents at Mussel Slough, with William R. Hearst's political ambitions serving as a later prod. Bierce's "all but forgotten contribution in singlehandedly defeating Huntington's unjust Funding Bill," he concludes, "was probably his greatest journalistic victory and an amazing testament to the power of his pen." At the same time, Bierce "managed to transcend the limits of reporting by injecting his own keen wit and satirical thrusts into his columns dealing with the railroad bloc."[23]

Morris correctly questions the success of Bierce's fight and notes the writer's ambivalence. The author of the most recently published Bierce biography emphasizes the 1896 "compromise amendment" by Congressman H. Henry Powers for an eighty-year repayment of the debt. Hearst, he points out, cynically trumpeted that political draw as "total victory." But Morris skims over the final settlement, which occurred in 1899 and came closer to real victory for Hearst. It forced the railroad to repay the money in ten years.[24]

Several historians and biographers offer passing but respectul mentions of Bierce's railroad work. Oscar Lewis's fluid account of the lives and machinations of "the Big Four" who ran the railroad—Huntington, Stanford, Charles Crocker, and Mark Hopkins—notes that Bierce had always taken pleasure in exposing the discomforts visited on passengers by the railroad, but that he began his attacks in earnest when he went to work for Hearst and was afforded the protection of wealth that could not be corrupted by the railroad's usual methods.[25] Robert A. Wiggins's slim biography contributes little to the literature, only suggesting that Bierce "returned home something of a hero."[26] C. Hartley Grattan adds little more than that the journalist was "severe on deliberate exploitation of employees or the general public and especially so on the hypocritical moral attitude of those who practiced exploitation," and that Bierce liked to call the industrialist Andrew Carnegie a "smugwump."[27] Franklin Walker, who describes the funding bill imbroglio as Bierce's "greatest opportunity as a fighting journalist," agrees that Bierce seems to have defeated it singlehandedly, but adds that "under other circumstances" Bierce might have "admired" the "ability" of Huntington, "whose social ideas agreed with many of his own."[28]

One of the most perceptive interpreters of Bierce's fiction and poetry unfortunately never addressed the railroad issue in depth. Mary E. Grenander mentions only that the funding bill fight was "a struggle of titans."[29] Her analysis of Bierce's short stories, however, gives some clues to his social concerns. His "didactic tales," such as "The Famous Gilson Bequest," rely on the thesis that individual human greed is nearly inevitable and that "when it permeates . . . society, it tears to pieces the fabric of organized living."[30] Other works of fiction written by Bierce require the reader to question accepted values, using three methods: "a reversal of genuine standards, hyperbolic exaggeration, or understatement." These "mimetic tales of action" always "present an outrageous and unqualified deflection from accepted norms by egocentric and amoral characters who are callously insensible to the finer emotions and who are motivated primarily by expediency, cupidity, or sadism, yet the reader reacts by asking himself how far the ordinarily unquestioned day-to-day practice also swerves from the standards to which society pays lip service."[31]

Bierce's antagonistic relationship with the railroad has also inspired at least one work of fiction, Oakley Hall's mystery novel *Ambrose Bierce and the Queen of Spades*. Based loosely on the historical feud between Bierce and the Big Four, the book provides a bloodless and occasionally inaccurate portrayal of the journalist and his railroad enemies and sheds little light on his aims or methods. It ends with a fictional rendering of the conventional historical wisdom, describing the funding bill fight as a grand victory for Bierce and his "final triumph over Huntington and the Railroad, which had been a long time coming."[32]

Far from acclaiming Bierce as a hero, three writers have questioned his attacks on the Central Pacific on the ground of his motivation, claiming that spite and wounded self-interest drove him to campaign against the railroad rather than any real concern for the commonweal. Two of these authors, however, were contemporaries who bore Bierce considerable ill will. The third wrote an admiring biography of Huntington.

Adolphe de Castro, who also had gone by the name of Alfred Danziger and who had followed a varied career—dentist, rabbi, and writer—was a friend of Bierce who collaborated with him on a book called *The Monk and the Hangman's Daughter*. But the two had quarreled over proceeds from the work. By one account, the friendship ended with Bierce breaking a cane over de Castro/Danziger's head. According to de Castro, Bierce hated the railroad and its officers because they had refused to give him a sort of public relations job after he returned to San Francisco from a mining venture in the Dakota Territory in 1880.[33]

Because of lingering resentment over the book dispute, de Castro's accuracy about details of Bierce's life has been questioned by McWilliams and many others. De Castro claims that Bierce offered the Big Four a proposal for colonizing the land opened up by the railroad—a weird and unlikely scheme, since much of the acreage bordered by its tracks consisted of practically uninhabitable mountains or desert. Bierce, the story continues, went away "elated" after speaking with Stanford and being promised a job. But later, waiting to meet with Stanford at the railroad's San Francisco offices at Fourth and Townsend, he became "an involuntary listener" to a discussion between Huntington and Stanford in an adjoining room. He is supposed to have heard Stanford broach the idea, and Huntington turn it down with the words:

"Forget it, Senator. When I want a scribbler, I'll hire one. This fellow is uncontrollable."

The dejected journalist would have committed suicide save for the family he had to support, according to de Castro. Bierce's primary interest in the job lay in getting an easy living so he could comfortably produce the fiction he really wanted to write. He remained embittered against Huntington and the railroad for the rest of his life because he could not support himself and his family in the style he had envisioned. He "felt the pinch of poverty more than once" during the next thirty years and had to borrow from de Castro occasionally.[34]

Bierce, according to this argument, lacked Hearst's "broad motives" for attacking Huntington and the railroad. It was merely a vendetta. According to de Castro, his former friend once declared that "a cause is always a venal thing. . . . Christ had no cause to fight for. Paul had. It was his business. A cause creates fanatics." De Castro suggests that Bierce's writing took on a "new and significant vigor" against the railroad when he went to work for Hearst in 1887—many years after the supposed rebuff by the railroad magnates—because the time was right for vengeance.[35]

Joseph Noel, a California newspaperman, playwright, and contemporary of Bierce, implies that an equally personal but somewhat less self-interested motive caused Bierce to take on Huntington. Noel claims that F. C. Havens, the uncle of one of Bierce's closest friends, the poet George Sterling, stood to benefit financially from the improvement of the fortunes of the Santa Fe Railroad, a competitor of the Southern Pacific. Havens held an interest in an East Bay railway that would serve as the terminus for the Santa Fe.

Bierce and Sterling became acquainted in the early 1890s, and this would suggest that, should Noel's charge be true, Bierce's attacks ought to have increased thereafter. They did in only one year, however— 1896, when Hearst sent Bierce to Washington specifically to file frequent dispatches on the funding bill debate. Elsewhere in his reminiscences, Noel, who apparently only met Bierce twice, contends that Bierce "humiliated" Huntington during the funding bill fight not because he wanted to reclaim money for the United States but because he sought the satisfaction of challenging and defeating authority, which he describes as the essence of Bierce's life and work.[36] This "sadistic compulsion" he attributes to an unhappy childhood when "nothing was spared to make the tousle-headed blond boy feel that he was a worm."[37] Although this analysis may be notable as an early application of a now-fashionable theory of popular psychology, it should be noted that Bierce devoted much of his writing during his last decade as a journalist to attacking socialists, of which Noel was one. Noel likely was trying to defend his own self-esteem as much as he was attempting to assess Bierce's.

In her laudatory biography of Huntington, Evans repeats de Castro's account of the failed public relations scheme and an ensuing lifelong lust for revenge on Bierce's part. Hearst, she continues, sent Bierce to Washington for the funding bill fight not to secure repayment of the bonds to the government but to bring about foreclosure and to make Huntington personally liable for the bonds. The funding bill fight was a defeat for Bierce because the railroad did not go into foreclosure and Huntington was not forced to dip into his personal fortune. This is a dubious interpretation, however, because the issue was being litigated and a decision by the United States Supreme Court eventually ruled out the issue of personal liability for the Big Four and their estates.

Nevertheless, Evans might agree that Bierce's conduct deserved to be called muckraking, at least in the pejorative sense intended by President Theodore Roosevelt in 1906 when he first applied the term to journalists. Bierce and "the Opposition" blackened Huntington's name through "storms of abuse, falsehood, and ridicule, [and] the missiles of venom and malevolence," a "serious and deplorable feature" not only for Huntington but for the generations that followed, "many of whom to this day [1954] mention his name sneeringly or with scorn."[38]

LIMITS OF BIOGRAPHY

Although he was a journalist for practically all of his working days, Bierce led a varied and complicated personal and professional life. In his time, he published not only a prolific amount of journalism ranging from satirical snippets to lengthy essays, but a great deal of fiction and poetry as well. Though he had a wife and three children, he lived apart from his family for much of the time. As restless physically as he was mentally, he punctuated the years with frequent moves, partly to seek respite from attacks of asthma that plagued him.

In some respects, Bierce is nearly impossible to see whole. A written record of his bylined newspaper pieces remains, but it is often a tangle of conflicting opinions. Read by posterity, "the Bierce thought is so full of contradictions that it seems less like thinking than like emotional caprice." In one place, he opposes widespread college education; in another, he supports it. Numerous other examples exist.[39]

He hated biographers, considering them to be little more than literary Peeping Toms. "Publication of letters not written for publication
is prima facie evidence of moral delinquency in the offender," he once
wrote.[40] It sometimes appears that he tried to cover the tracks left from
his own life, as Paul Fatout, among others, has pointed out.[41] He was
"frightfully honest" about others but he was "not publicly truthful about
himself," McWilliams has noted. Not surprisingly, much of the written
commentary on him can be summed up as a "maze of conjecture and
hearsay" and a "Library of Error."[42]

Descriptions of Bierce by friends, acquaintances, and family often are conflicting, protective, or evasive. Mrs. Ruth Guthrie Harding
likened her garden walks with him to "strolling with St. Francis of
Assisi,"[43] while Neale, his long-time publisher, remembered him as
"selfish, self-centered, and never given to self-abnegation."[44]

Some years after Bierce's disappearance, most likely in Mexico,
a researcher tracked down his daughter, Helen, then living in Los Angeles and operating a secretarial school. She refused to give many details
of her father's life, suggesting that her interviewer limit his inquiries to
studying her father's published work (and leading the suspicious sleuth
to hatch an odd theory, one of many rising from the ashes of Bierce's
mysterious disappearance, that she was trying to cover up Ambrose's
incarceration in an insane asylum in Napa, California).[45] Later, remi-
niscing about her father in an article in the *American Mercury*, Helen
indulged herself in some not uncommon hagiography: Ambrose Bierce
walks into a clearing, raises his hands to the sky in an ethereal gesture,
and the very birds flock to him unafraid.[46]

Despite her understandable inclination to idealize her father,
Helen had a point. As one critic has written, too many biographers have
fixed their gaze on Bierce's strange and macabre character. (Mencken
reports, for instance, that Bierce, whom he knew late in Bierce's life,
kept an urn containing a dead son's ashes on his desk for use as an
ashtray.) They thereby have missed what one critic has called "the
steady luminosity"[47] of his work and failed to understand "Bierce in his
brilliant obscurity."[48]

Bierce as a journalistic force at times nearly equaled the railroad
as a political force. The queer theories and anecdotes surrounding his
life often have led to the mistaken conviction that he was "a second-rate
individual and a hack journalist."[49] In fact, his journalism "constitutes
one of the most extensive and able critiques of America in print"[50] and
"constantly surprises new generations with its freshness, lucidity, and
timelessness."[51]

SOURCES

When one considers that his newspaper and magazine work spanned forty-two years and two continents, it becomes less surprising that the opinions Bierce expressed in his work sometimes appear contradictory. He produced thousands of columns and articles, usually writing one or more a week for more than thirty years. He interrupted his weekly column, called "Prattle" for much of its existence, only for sickness, vacations, and occasional journalistic tangents such as the funding bill fight and a challenge to the Spanish-American War, which he called the "Yanko-Spanko" war.

Some of those columns have been collected in his twelve-volume *Collected Works*, a set of tomes that critics agree would have benefited from heavy editing by someone other than Bierce.[52] Even so, the *Works* represent only a small fraction of his total output. From a historical perspective, his journalistic material in the books can be of limited value. He edited and reworked much of it in the last few years before his disappearance. In spite of the existence of the voluminous *Works*, most of his journalism went uncollected and must be mined in the dark recesses of microfilm rooms. Even here, the evidence is not complete, since individual issues of magazines like the *Wasp* and the *Argonaut* often are missing from university collections.

Still, a reading of most of his newspaper work is necessary to understand how his antagonism to the railroad began, if not necessarily why, and how it changed, not only in content but in style. Such research not only answers the charges of contemporaries like de Castro, but shows whether and how Bierce's ideas changed over time and how his methods compared to those of the muckrakers he was sometimes said to have inspired.

The years under study run from Bierce's employment on the *Argonaut*, beginning in 1877, to 1901, a year after Huntington, the last surviving member of the Big Four, died, when Bierce was writing less energetically for Hearst's newspapers and magazines. The study will not review Bierce's early work on the *San Francisco News-Letter* because the railroad was still in its infancy. Bierce's early freelancing, his work for British periodicals such as Tom Hood's *Fun* and American newspapers such as the *New York Journal*, and his writing for the *San Francisco Examiner* after 1901 likewise will not be examined because they are unlikely to yield much railroad material.

His work in *Cosmopolitan* from 1905 to 1909 will be discussed briefly, however, because *Cosmopolitan* was an important muckraking magazine and because Bierce's "Small Contributions" (a name for his occasional column for the magazine) shed some light on his hostility to muckrakers and reformers. Also, it represented his journalistic last gasp. After he quit writing for *Cosmopolitan* in 1909, he published no new material but continued to gather and edit material for his *Collected Works* before disappearing in Mexico.

To answer another question, that raised by Bierce's style of personal journalism and his success in wounding Collis P. Huntington, a similar path can be taken. Although much railroad material is stored in the Huntington Library in San Marino, California, the library has proved to be somewhat jealous of its possessions.[53] But a good collection of Huntington's letters, as they passed through his Wall Street office, is available to the public on microfilm. The collection includes numerous reels—one hundred and fifteen, each containing hundreds of letters and other documents—but two offer key material relating not only to the funding bill, but to Huntington's overall press strategy in California. They include many letters between Huntington and his chief California press manipulator, William H. Mills. These letters—Huntington's in longhand, Mills's usually composed on a typewriter—not only give an indication of how Huntington played the press, but also help evaluate Bierce's success in vanquishing this rotund, platitude-spouting railroad dragon.

Finally, Bierce's personal letters offer some clues to his own satisfaction and dissatisfaction with the results of his attacks on the railroad. Unfortunately, many of his letters have been lost, and those known to be in existence are scattered in libraries across the country. Grenander has pointed out that the bulk of the material relevant to the railroad fight is at Stanford University.[54] (It is a vindication of McWilliams's comment on the limited effects of Bierce's satire that many of his letters and documents now reside in libaries that carry the surnames of his two greatest railroad enemies, Huntington and Stanford; it should be noted, however, that the Huntington was named for Collis's nephew, who, some years after his uncle's death, married his uncle's widow and thereby reunited the family fortune. It should also be mentioned that librarians at Stanford have been entirely accommodating in providing public access to Bierce artifacts.)

The collection at Stanford's Green Library contains no letters from Bierce concerning the railroad or the funding bill fight, but it does include many letters and telegrams sent to Bierce by Hearst editors during the heat of the battle. Some of these shed light on the methods and

motives of Bierce and the *Examiner*. Also, some of his published letters, particularly those printed by the Book Club of California, will be
consulted, not because they illuminate his stance on the railroad—they
do not—but because they vent his feelings later in his career about reform and journalism.[55]

NOTES

1. Many historical accounts of the railroad's power in California exist. See, for example, Oscar Lewis, *The Big Four* (New York: Alfred A. Knopf, 1969) or Walton Bean and James J. Rawls, *California: An Interpretive History*, 4th ed. (New York: McGraw-Hill Book Co., 1983), 245–254.

2. Carey McWilliams, *Ambrose Bierce: A Biography* (New York: Albert & Charles Boni, 1929), 158.

3. See, for example, Fremont Older, *My Own Story* (San Francisco: The Call Publishing Co., 1919).

4. Cerinda W. Evans, *Collis Potter Huntington,* 2 vols. (Newport News, Virginia: The Mariners' Museum, 1954). The Mariners' Museum was founded and funded in 1930 by Collis P. Huntington's son, Archer M. Huntington.

5. Ernest Jerome Hopkins, "Bierce, Hearst, and the 'Rail-Rogue' Battle" (faculty research project, Arizona State University, Tempe, Arizona, 1967), and Hopkins, ed., *The Ambrose Bierce Satanic Reader* (New York: Doubleday & Co., 1968).

6. The articles eventually were collected in a book: Charles Edward Russell, *Railroad Melons, Rates and Wages: A Handbook of Railroad Information* (Chicago: Charles H. Kerr & Co., 1922).

7. Hopkins, 30, from Russell, *Melons*, 143.

8. Russell, *Melons*, 142–145.

9. Fremont Older, *Growing Up* (San Francisco: San Francisco Call-Bulletin, 1931), 146.

10. Hopkins, 30.

11. Hopkins, ed., *The Ambrose Bierce Satanic Reader*, 194.

12. McWilliams, 245.

13. Ibid., 239.

14. Ibid., 244.

15. Lawrence I. Berkove, "Ambrose Bierce's Concern with Mind and Man" (Ph.D. dissertation, University of Pennsylvania, 1962), 27.

16. Lawrence I. Berkove, "The Man with the Burning Pen: Ambrose Bierce as Journalist." *Journal of Popular Culture*, 15 (1981), 38.

17. Janet M. Francendese, "Ambrose Bierce as Journalist" (Ph.D. dissertation, New York University, 1977), 32.

18. Ibid., 201.

19. Richard O'Connor, *Ambrose Bierce: A Biography* (Boston: Little. Brown & Co., 1967), 227.

20. Ibid., 237.

21. Walter Neale, *Life of Ambrose Bierce* (New York: Walter Neale, 1929), 95–96.

22. Richard Saunders, *Ambrose Bierce: The Making of a Misanthrope* (San Francisco: Chronicle Books, 1985), 33–36.

23. Ibid., 71.

24. Roy Morris, Jr., *Ambrose Bierce: Alone in Bad Company* (New York: Crown Publishers, 1995), 226.

25. Lewis, 350.

26. Robert A. Wiggins, *Ambrose Bierce* (Minneapolis: University of Minnesota Press, 1964), 38.

27. C. Hartley Grattan, *Bitter Bierce: A Mystery of American Letters* (New York: Doubleday, 1929), 216.

28. Franklin Walker, *Ambrose Bierce: The Wickedest Man in San Francisco* (San Francisco: The Colt Press, 1941), 15.

29. Mary E. Grenander, *Ambrose Bierce* (New York: Twayne Publishers, 1971), 56–57.

30. Ibid., 89

31. Ibid., 132.

32. Oakley Hall, *Ambrose Bierce and the Queen of Spades* (Berkeley: University of California Press, 1998).

33. Adolphe de Castro, *Portrait of Ambrose Bierce* (New York: The Century Co., 1929), 56, 237.

34. Ibid., 56.

35. Ibid., 116–117.

36. Joseph Noel, *Footloose in Arcadia* (New York: Carrick & Evans, 1940), 69.

37. Ibid., 68.

38. Evans, 479–493.

39. Paul Fatout, *The Devil's Lexicographer* (Norman: University of Oklahoma Press, 1956), 48.

40. Ambrose Bierce, *The Collected Works of Ambrose Bierce*, 12 vols. (New York: The Neale Publishing Co., 1909–1912), 11:394.

41. Paul Fatout, *Ambrose Bierce and the Black Hills* (Norman: University of Oklahoma Press, 1956), 48.

42. McWilliams, 5–8, 141.

43. Ibid., 307.

44. Neale, 222.

45. The anecdote is contained in unpublished "Notes on Bierce" taken by the novelist Paul Jordan Smith and contained in the Bierce collection at the Green Library, Stanford University.

46. Helen Bierce, "Ambrose Bierce at Home," *American Mercury*, 30 (December 1933): 455.

47. Wilson Follett, "Ambrose, Son of Marcus Aurelius," *Atlantic Monthly* (July 1937): 32.

48. Wilson Follett, "Bierce in His Brilliant Obscurity," *New York Times*, 11 October 1936, 6:2.

49. McWilliams, 8.

50. Berkove, *Popular Culture*, 37.

51. Follett, *Atlantic Monthly*, 38.

52. See, for instance, H. L. Mencken, *A Mencken Chrestomathy* (New York: Alfed A. Knopf, 1949), 492, and Follett, *Atlantic Monthly*, 35.

53. Personal letter from Kathy Schneberger, Library Assistant, Huntington Library, to author, 13 April 1992. The library did make available by mail

some photocopied Bierce and Huntington letters, which proved not to be relevant to the topic at hand.

54. Personal letter from M. E. Grenander to author, 28 March 1992.

55. Bertha Pope Clark, ed., *The Letters of Ambrose Bierce* (San Francisco: The Book Club of California, 1922).

3

Muckrakers

Bierce's reputation as a cynic makes it a formidable task to classify him as a muckraker. If one attempts to compromise and conclude that he was some combination of the two, how can such seemingly opposite worldviews be reconciled?

An examination of his methods, style, and fortunes shows that he did indeed anticipate the muckrakers. The similarities in their means and ends—and the divergences—say something not only about Bierce and later muckrakers but also about the "literature of exposure" as a whole.

Such a classification entails at least a brief definition of muckraking as historians have attempted to classify it. It also provokes an inquiry into Bierce's motivations. Was he, in his duel with Huntington, public-minded, which at least on the face of things would suggest a muckraking definition? Or did he attack the railroad out of spite, ambition, or merely the duty of the loyal newspaper employee? Historians' assessments of the muckraking era help form a definition of the journalistic style, as do the autobiographies of several muckrakers, including two who, like Bierce, sought to expose the abuses of great railroad corporations.

INTERPRETATIONS OF BIERCE'S JOURNALISTIC AIMS AND METHODS

What were the style and content of Bierce's journalism, and what were its effects? Though his success certainly cannot be quantified, hints can be obtained from his own comments on the matter and from the observations of contemporaries and historians. Understanding not only his success, but its limits, helps place him in the muckraking tradition and aids in comprehending his own individualistic brand of journalism and the changes he made in it near the end of his recorded days. It also indicates the limits of journalistic effectiveness as a whole.

Some dissertationists have discerned a pattern in Bierce's journalism. He hoped in his newspaper writing not to expose and bring down groups, generalities, or abstractions, but instead targeted particular individuals, in his thinking the building blocks of institutions and corporations, just as soldiers make up armies. Individuals also were the most likely to be reached by journalistic attacks, since the public, in Bierce's view, read newspapers and magazines mainly for entertainment:

Remember that what you want is not so much to disclose his [an opponent's] meanness to the reader (who cares nothing about it) as to make him disclose it to your private discernment. . . . You are one of two gladiators in the arena: your first duty is to amuse the multitude. But as the multitude is not going to remember, after leaving the show, who is victorious, it is not worth while to take any hurts for a merely visible advantage. So fight as to prove to yourself that you are the abler swordsman—that is, the more honorable one. Victory in that is important, for it is lasting . . . and it is enjoyed ever afterward whenever you see or think of the vanquished.[1]

Bierce's journalism, Francendese suggests, is "narrow" and "fixed . . . on the sinner rather than on the sin." The particular issue, in fact, is less important than "the exposure of dishonesty, the disgrace of one's opponent." According to Francendese's interpretation, Bierce fashioned his journalism for his own satisfaction, mainly to be derived from humbling his enemies. The promise of social betterment was secondary: "Public disgrace is unnecessary. It is enough that the loser become aware of his own immorality. Bierce leaves it to us to understand that self-awareness precedes repentance, and repentance precedes reform."[2]

Neale foreshadows Francendese's observation a bit more glumly when he argues that Bierce's sinners are beyond forgiveness.[3] To seek absolution is "contemptible and cowardly" and to offer it, beyond the powers of mortal man.[4] McWilliams, too, notes the individualistic attacks of Bierce, but does not link them with his attempts at a general critique of society, which in any case he labels "not effective."[5] As for Bierce's journalism, particularly his satire while editor of the *Wasp*, McWilliams is "impressed with its futility." The style damaged Bierce's thinking by immersing him in petty quarrels and rages while failing to afflict his opponents' consciences. Bierce's problem was that even though he was "correct in his conclusions" and "anticipated modern thought," he lacked the tools of "modern investigation."[6]

Some critics have concluded that Bierce wasted his ample satirical talents on petty targets, in effect obliterating squirrels with an elephant gun.[7] Others have found his failing in the mode of expression itself—the "steam heat of journalism," as one dismissed it.[8] But with the railroad in his sights, Bierce clearly was hunting bigger game. He had spent much of his time in San Francisco as a sort of connoisseur of human deceits, attacking with insatiable gusto the city's pettifoggers and mountebanks and scoundrels as well as the merely vain or artistically inept. As a weekly columnist, he necessarily flitted from one victim to the next. But his assault on the railroad was woven through his journalism.

The subject was not petty. Railroads were one of the overriding issues of the day, not only economically and politically, but symbolically. For perceptive observers like Henry Adams, "the generation between 1865 and 1895 was already mortgaged to the railways, and no one knew it better than the generation itself."[9] What had begun as a technological innovation filled with the promise not only of boosting the economy but uniting and civilizing the country had turned into a disillusioning, intractable, ugly problem that seemed not only to corrupt the political process but to splinter groups by region and by class.

Barely twenty years after they began pushing for the Pacific road, the four one-time Sacramento merchants who controlled it had seen their combined net worth grow from $250,000 to $100 million or more. They made their political influence felt with velvet-gloved fists in ten western states and territories. Thanks to federal subsidies, the Big Four controlled 5,000 miles of track and 50 million acres of land.[10]

Warren Theodore Francke has noted in his study of the origins of muckraking that the strict definition of the genre is limited by time, medium, and style. As usually defined, it is a type of exposure with an emphasis on a reporter's investigation rather than on editorial outcry, taking place between 1902 and 1912 or 1914, and appearing in popular magazines. But he challenges much of that definition, arguing that muckraking is a function of journalistic style and method rather than of time and medium. The muckraking of the early twentieth century was not an innovation, he argues. Rather, he traces its beginnings to the middle of the nineteenth century.[11]

DEFINITIONS

Authors have struggled to define the meaning of muckraking, and a broad if amorphous body of definitions exists. A working definition of muckraking entails not only amassing useful elements but discarding those that have lost their worth.

Francke has perhaps done the most service in refining the definition, either stretching or breaking the boundaries of each limit.[12] He questions the "sharp break," time-bound concept in which it is argued that the large funds committed to early twentieth-century muckraking gave it a kind of critical mass that made it the only journalistic episode worthy of the name. He shows that much time and money had been devoted to the swill milk exposures published decades earlier and cites John G. Clark's count of 925 reform articles printed in six monthlies in the two decades prior to the conventionally defined muckraking era as evidence of earlier muckraking.[13]

Francke also refines and extends the concept of muckraking technique, concluding that it is "the effective combination of reportorial investigation and narrative style." This method was in use long before the arrival of twentieth-century muckrakers, beginning with James Gordon Bennett's *New York Herald* in 1836 and continuing with the *New York Times* and the *New York Tribune*, among others, in the 1870s. He points out that there is little justification for separating newspapers and magazines. Though the medium may differ, there is little difference in length, tone, or style.[14] (In Bierce's case, the difference in medium is even hazier: though historians are fond of calling Bierce's *Wasp* a magazine, the editors themselves always referred to it as a newspaper. Much of his fiction, a form now typically associated with magazines, originally appeared in newspapers.)

Louis Filler, too, has noted that muckraking did not begin with turn-of-the-century reform writers. These journalists attracted notice by their sheer numbers and output. They added, compared to earlier investigative writers, "an expression of popular will." Rather than unearthing causes, they merely satisfied public demand for an airing of political and social problems that were already well known. Although they helped focus and "precipitate" public opinion, they essentially followed rather than led it: "The competent muckraker would know how to bring his readers back to themselves, help them align themselves with the best in government and society, teach them to despise demagogues and self-pitying rascals."[15]

Twentieth-century muckrakers' propensity to advance alongside the ranks of an outraged citizenry rather than in the vanguard lent them part of their seeming political power and popularity. S. S. McClure, editor of *McClure's*, the foremost muckraking magazine of the early twentieth century, followed a "simple formula," according to Ray Stannard Baker, one of his leading reporters. McClure, considered a pioneer of twentieth-century muckraking, "told people more about things of which they were already hearing a good deal."[16] Profit as well as altruism guided McClure and the editors of competing magazines who soon began imitating his winning formula.[17] When the muckraking movement began to die—by one account, not because of counterattacks by big business but simply because public demand had given out when readers became tired of "shrill-voiced criticism"[18]—these same magazines abandoned political causes and filled their pages with fiction and stories about beautiful women and successful men.[19]

Although muckraking popularly is associated with radicalism, that view is oversimplified. Muckraking contains some surprisingly conservative elements. Many muckrakers professed a moderate stance in their reminiscences. In his autobiography, Baker concludes that Americans had been well aware of political corruption long before the turn of the century; the muckrakers' real contribution had been in documenting lawlessness rather than in exposing it. He scoffs at "portentously serious books discussing the so-called 'literature of exposure'" and descriptions of himself as "a flaming crusader," and objects that he "did not want to reform the world" but merely to "understand" it.[20] Many other muckrakers' autobiographies make similar objections.[21] Baker's article on the Northern Pacific Railroad in the 20 November 1901 issue of *Collier's Weekly*, sometimes called the first muckraking article, did not lash out at the trusts, but was "respectful and even partial to them."[22]

Trusts usually provided the material for muckrakers, but potential material seemed to be everywhere, especially if one accepts a wider time frame for muckraking: topics included exposures of swill milk made from distillery leavings in the 1850s, penal corruption, sweatshops, women's rights, and what were then called "Negro rights" (addressed in often bigoted articles with titles such as "The Negro Problem"). The muckrakers did not always take on what in today's terms would be "liberal" targets. One of Baker's first big muckraking articles for *McClure's*,

"The Right to Work," examined the bullying of nonstriking coalworkers in Pennsylvania by members of the United Mine Workers labor union.

Railroads were attacked not only for their own corruption and unfairness but also because they were crucial to the success of the manufacturing trusts. Deals often existed between the two, granting favorable rates to big shippers at the expense of smaller ones. As the arteries of the new industrial organism, railroads took a position in muckraking second only to that of its degenerate heart, the trusts themselves.

Charles Edward Russell, whose father had lost his newspaper in Davenport, Iowa, after daring to attack the railroads, produced 150 railroad articles in ten years.[23] Like another muckraker, Ida Tarbell, he believed that control of the railroads was the basis of the trusts' power, and that the railroads and the trusts were intimately connected: railroad rebates for dominant shippers played to the advantage of big companies like Standard Oil.[24]

In Baker's mind, the "railroad problem" was closely linked to the struggle between capital and labor. In 1905, as he worked on "Railroads on Trial," his series of muckraking railroad exposés for *McClure's*, he "read everything he could get [his] hands on," though he does not mention Bierce's attacks on the Central Pacific.[25] Bierce likewise does not appear in Russell's autobiography although he is mentioned in one of his collected articles.

Although Baker favored regulation as a way of reining in the railroads' rates, others, like Russell, saw government takeover as the only likely solution. Some held little hope at all for betterment but were still muckrakers. Alfred Henry Lewis, an individualistic, proud man who left early careers as a lawyer and cattleman to expose railroads, trusts, and corrupt politicians when he later became a muckraker for Hearst, "despised Socialism" and "had no faith in reform."[26]

Even when the railroads were not the focus of muckrakers' investigations, they often were tied to other culprits. David Graham Phillips charged that "every traitor senator, whatever else he represents in the way of an enemy to the people, always represents some thief or groups of thieves through railways."[27]

Criticism and exposure of railroads had existed long before the twentieth-century muckrakers. Charles Francis Adams, brother of Henry and the "grandfather" of muckraking, had earned that title with an attack on the Erie Railroad a few years after the Civil War. B. O. Flower, son of a midwestern minister of the Disciples of Christ who had considered following his father's calling but instead had become a Unitarian and crusading journalist, carried on an anti-railroad campaign in his *Arena* throughout the 1890s and summed it up in a July 1904 article bluntly headlined "Twenty Five Years of Bribery and Corrupt Practices."

But Flower, in one historian's estimation, was not so much an activist as a "word monger." Like many other reform-minded journalists who had become active in the 1890s, his journalism functioned more as academic exercise than as political thrust. In this view, much of the reform journalism of the 1890s had been a parade of angst, so much intellectual shadow-boxing, obsessed with the world as it should be while overlooking things as they were and reasonably might be. Many of these journalists were the middle-class sons of ministers who became "theoretical socialists and practical aristocrats."[28]

A decade later, the socialist Russell believed that government regulation would not be sufficient to tame the rapacity of the railroads. Even the milder Baker was forced to admit that regulation was probably not sufficient. Baker's articles, while they spurred the Congress and President Theodore Roosevelt to promulgate more effective railroad regulation, were in many ways equivocal. So judicious are many of his pieces that they detract somewhat from Francke's central-villain concept in his muckraking formula. Roosevelt, having read Baker's series and solicited his suggestions for tackling the problem, commended him on his even-handedness: "One of the lessons you teach is that the railroad men are not to be treated as villains but merely as ordinary Americans, who under given conditions are by the mere force of events forced into doing much of which we complain."[29]

Although some muckrakers, like Russell and Upton Sinclair, were socialists, most were not. George E. Mowry maintains that the Progressive movement was in some respects a conservative backlash of middle-class, religious, midwestern, Protestant, college-educated men from old American families, descendants of an "old aristocracy" rooted in Puritan New England, who feared that the industrial and social changes sweeping across the country were causing "many of society's rewards and badges of merit" to go to others. Elsewhere, he suggests that their opposition to the trusts and railroads represented not a protest against private property, but an individualistic revolt against corporate concentration. The muckrakers' view of the problem tended to be colored by individualism, too, and was highly particular. They distinguished between "good and bad wealth" and "good and bad trusts." Unlike earlier reform movements of Grangers and Populists, the Progressive movement and muckraking tended to be centered in the cities rather than in the countryside.[30]

Like Mowry, Richard E. Hofstadter identifies a prevailing midwestern, Protestant background as a central trait of the muckrakers, in one place going so far as to describe progressivism as tantamount to a "latter-day Protestant revival." He also describes muckraking as a middle-class reaction to a changing order and draws a distinction between muckraking after the turn of the century and the journalistic exposure of the 1890s by pointing to muckraking's wider audience.[31]

The muckrakers' private lives often seemed to conflict with their public mien. Even so violently rebellious a muckraker as Phillips, "theoretically a democrat, . . . was always an aristocrat in practice."[32] Their targets also could be diverse. Articles attacked corrupt unions as well as corrupt railroads and trusts. The socialist movement "supplemented" muckraking but was not integral to it.[33] In recounting an amiable argument he had with the socialist writer Jack London, Baker is careful to set himself apart not only from London's socialism but from the even milder label of reformer also:

'You see, I'm not a reformer. I'm a reporter. . . . I'm not sure yet that if either you or I made over the world, it would be any better than the one we now have. We don't know enough.' . . . The difference between us lay probably in the fact that he wanted to reform me, and I did not want to reform him.[34]

In her autobiography, Ida Tarbell also retreated from an activist label: "My point of attack has always been that of a journalist after the fact, rarely that of a reformer."[35] And though the Carnegies, Rockefellers, and Goulds she exposed had been motivated by selfish and often "sinister" interest, they also had "contributed to higher living standards and hurried on the nationalization of the country."[36] Later, Filler characterized muckrakers like Finley Peter Dunne as "simple" and "hopeful" men who "planned no diabolical revolutions."[37]

Many muckrakers saw their journalism as an almost religious mission. Men like Jacob Riis and William Stead, one the son of a preacher, the other of a professor, were "born again" into journalism as a means of reform beyond the pulpit.[38] Baker recounts his conversion to muckraking as an almost religious experience. He hears the call while practically wandering in the desert. After a winter of ennui and discontent while on a New Mexico ranch in 1901 where, exhausted and depressed from overwork, he is attempting to regather his physical and mental strength, he begins to revive: "It was something like an old-fashioned religious conversion. I had such a sense of conviction and inner unity, a new purpose in life, as I had never felt before." His "duty," he had decided, was to explain to his fellow Americans, long accustomed to the luxury of wide-open spaces, "the art of living in a crowded world."[39]

Muckrakers often portrayed themselves as optimistic and altruistic, and historians seldom have argued the point. "We 'muckraked' not because we hated our world but because we loved it," Baker wrote. "We were not cynical, we were not hopeless, we were not bitter."[40]

"Personally astonished, personally ashamed, personally indignant at what we found," he explained, he and his fellow muckrakers naturally wrote "hotly."[41]

MUCKRAKING METHODS

Muckrakers have relied on a variety of means for accomplishing their ends. Francke has identified satire as one literary method in nineteenth-century muckraking. Its use was common in such pieces in *Harper's Weekly* and the *North American Review* in the 1860s. Often, so bitter a medicine was administered sparingly and in dilute form. Typically, the ironist within the muckraker eventually yielded to "clinical reporter and then outraged humanist."[42]

It was indeed a mild form of satire. Charles Francis Adams's attack on the machinations of the Erie Railroad in the *North American Review* in 1869 was "more patronizing than bitter."[43] But it was not unusual. Henry Demarest Lloyd, a preacher's son who exposed the Standard Oil Trust in the 1880s and published *Wealth Against Commonwealth* in 1894, used liberal amounts of irony and satire in his work.

One of the ways in which later muckrakers' methods differed from those of nineteenth-century muckrakers was in the later reporters' spotlighting of a central villain. Lloyd's work did not name Rockefeller.[44] Adams's exposure of the Erie Railroad used "comparable" and even "less sophisticated" narrative techniques.[45] The "well-unified narrative" of later muckraking was usually "created by a single prominent reporter who to some degree became the protagonist."[46] A Fisk, an Armour, a Rockefeller, or similar antagonist often was the focus of later muckrakers' efforts. These rogue millionaires lent the articles in which they appeared a literary form and narrative power.

Even so, Baker finally was to lament that muckraking articles amounted to a kind of two-dimensional caricature. The pork-packing baron Philip Armour had pointed out during an interview that, had he stepped aside, some other industrialist would have replaced him and engaged in the same questionable practices. Baker expressed regret that he had not got to know Armour better so he could have shown more clearly "the human side of the problems" and that Armour was "a mere man, like the rest of us."[47]

Some historians have detected two sorts of muckraking method—one based on painstaking, investigative research and another more literary and "impressionistic."[48] The latter method, often "full of sound and fury," is attributed to writers like David Graham Phillips and his occasionally wild attacks on the United States Senate. But the literary component of muckraking also has a more positive quality that is often cited although more difficult to pin down.

Many of the muckrakers were poets *manqués*. Russell was "a proud, sensitive man who yearned romantically to accomplish worthwhile things."[49] Most of the muckrakers of the 1900s had been newspaper reporters and editors in the 1890s and had learned that the literary fruits of toiling in the newspaper vineyard were minimal.[50] Arthur Brisbane, a high Hearst editor and columnist, perhaps summed up the prevailing insiders' view of the depth of the medium when he advised a young newspaper recruit: "If you would succeed in journalism, never lose your superficiality."[51]

Filler goes so far as to distinguish the magazine muckraking of the 1900s from the newspaper yellow journalism of the previous decade by exclaiming that "muckraking was literary rather than 'yellow'!" This distinction manifested itself not only in style and in medium, but in scope. Yellow journalism was written by local news-hounds about local scandals. It was designed for "quick reading" and "quick results." Muckrakers, on the other hand, were "fully informed, fully rounded men capable of expressing and interpreting large sectors of the national life as they had found it."[52]

Filler counts William Randolph Hearst as "the soil, or the subsoil, of the muckraking movement," even though Hearst's *San Francisco Examiner*, and more especially his *New York Journal*, became paragons of yellow journalism as their new publisher attempted to breathe life into those listless sheets.[53] As an undergraduate at Harvard, Hearst had neglected his course work but avidly studied the newspapers of that leading yellow journalist, Joseph Pulitzer. (Hearst later acquired the *New York Journal* from Pulitzer's brother.) Filler points out that many muckrakers, such as Tarbell, Russell, London, Lewis, Henry George, Sinclair, and others, wrote not only for Hearst's "yellow" newspapers but also for his muckraking magazine, *Cosmopolitan*.[54]

The difference between a "muckraker" like Hearst and a "yellow journalist" like Pulitzer, according to Filler, is that Hearst swam with the tide of muckraking and "flourished more than ever."[55] The distinction seems to be more of time than of method. Francke declares that yellow journalism is merely a concept defined by time, and discerns little difference between it and muckraking.[56] Both types of journalism shared "scene-setting traits" and gave readers an "eyewitness tour" of the problems they sought to illuminate. Hearst and Pulitzer merely followed a journalistic tradition based on the exploits of reporters like Julius Chambers, who in 1872, while a reporter for the *New York Tribune*, feigned madness and "went among the maniacs" to expose the cruel conditions of insane asylums. Hearst and Pulitzer even shared a common shortcoming—they exposed dire social effects but tended to ignore their causes.[57]

Because of their preoccupation with central villains and protagonists, each story became a small, particular drama. The muckrakers could expose bad situations but seldom could devise an overall critique of a system that fostered such problems. Their independence and individualism, however, did not mean they stood aloof from politics.[58] The most effective journalistic reform attempts were always aligned with a popular movement. The muckrakers reflected the concerns of the Progressives in the new century. In the preceding decade, reformers like Lloyd were aligned with the Populists.

But connections with new political parties did not override the muckrakers' fundamental faith in individual solutions. They had grown up in an environment that espoused individualism and they expected the nation to right itself the same way. "If this republic is to be saved," Baker wrote in a muckraking article on corrupt unions in 1903, "it must be saved by individual effort."[59] Lincoln Steffens counted on the civic pride of the individual to put things right, and one of Tarbell's main gripes in her exposure of Standard Oil was that small producers were being trampled.[60]

EFFECTS OF MUCKRAKING

The seeming paradox of social consciousness combined with devout individualism did produce concrete results, though the muckrakers did not get all they had hoped for.[61] Their wishes were too numerous, too new, and too diverse to come true. And some problems, even after years of attack, did not seem as amenable to correction as once supposed. As Baker anguished in his autobiography: "What *would* the money-changers do after they were driven out? Where were the followers of Jesus who would keep them out by devising a better way of life and practicing it themselves? And what was the better way of life?"[62]

From Baker's time as a muckraker back to the attacks on the Erie Railroad in 1869, a common complaint about journalistic exposure had been that it was unnecessary. The public was well aware of corruption, it was argued, and exposure served no purpose.[63] But muckraking in the first decade of the twentieth century did help bring about real change, including direct election of United States senators, women's suffrage, the initiative and referendum, and serious attempts at regulating business.

The muckrakers not only helped win individual battles, but bore responsibility at least in part for rallying the country around a cause. Unlike many of the reform journalists of the 1890s—"essentially, a story of failure"[64]—the muckrakers of the following decade definitely affected practical politics. By 1906, the federal government had at least begun to wield something approaching real regulatory power over railroads and the manufacture of food and drugs, thanks to the muckrakers (and sometimes to their partial dismay, as with Sinclair's *The Jungle*, intended as a socialist jeremiad but interpreted by many in and outside the government as a call for laws safeguarding the purity of food).[65]

Baker and others believed that their work had helped the public support the progressive agenda of Theodore Roosevelt and other politicians.[66] Despite his success as a muckraker, when Baker looked back on his achievements decades later, it was with some skepticism. He lamented Americans' "pathetic faith" in statutes, initiatives, and referenda as solutions. "There may be considerable education of individual minds in the process of campaigning for such reforms," he concluded, "but it is astonishing how little, how very little, they change actual conditions."[67]

Tarbell's assessment was somewhat brighter, though she seemed to agree that muckraking's effects had been exaggerated. "In our eagerness to find the true solution," she wrote in her autobiography, "we failed to inquire why this same solution failed to work when tried before—for it always had been tried before, even if we in our self-confidence did not know it." She did allow, however, that the cycles of history, while they turned on and on, did so in an ever "upward spiral."[68]

David Mark Chalmers cites three main achievements for muckraking: generating public awareness of pervasive corruption in American politics and society, providing an understanding that each case was related and formed a discomforting tableau of "the malfunction of American society," and explaining that power had been dangerously concentrated in the industrial oligarchies rising in the wake of the agrarian age.[69]

A major flaw of the muckrakers, according to Tebbel, was that they lacked a grand vision and that they dwelt "on sickness, not possible cures."[70] Chalmers, in fact, asserts that their articles did not solve the problems they revealed and concludes that their biggest success was in having developed "a new form of detailed, factual, investigatory journalism," an assertion that, given the work of Francke and others, is suspect.[71]

In fact, the muckrakers' failure to achieve total success was no stranger than the supposedly "new" style of journalism they practiced. Upton Sinclair's *Jungle* may have spurred improvements in packing plants and factories, but it no more guaranteed pure food than state laws guaranteed pure milk following the swill milk exposures of the 1850s.[72] In recent times, innovations such as the initiative have not always been used in the progressive ways imagined by their originators.

Though hopeful, the muckrakers were scarcely naive enough to believe themselves capable of complete success. When Baker arrived in New York City to launch his muckraking career after his sojourn in the New Mexico desert, he carried with him his "now indispensable *Meditations of Marcus Aurelius*." It is not likely he read the pessimistic writings of the Stoic philosopher and emperor with a view to unconditional victory.[73] Looking back at the period, he detected in the intervening decades "superficial improvements . . . in the conditions we reported," but "sadly" conceded that "the deeper-seated injustices remain, still unpurged."[74]

As a muckraker who was also a socialist, Charles Edward Russell had to declare that muckraking was "wholesome" but "just one more experiment in symptom dosing," a futile practice that does "nothing against the fundamental system that is the source of our troubles."[75] Historians often seem to echo Russell's plaints, although with varying degrees of fervor and sometimes without the implication that socialism was the only path out. One of the more pessimistic assessments concluded that "nearly every one of these reforms . . . remains more or less unrealized."[76]

The muckrakers shared in many cases a common background: an almost religious faith in not only the necessity of reform but in the possibility of it. The weapons they used to unmask evil-doing were often as literary as they were journalistic, relying on narrative, in-depth studies of particular corporate villains and sometimes including small doses of satire. They exposed problems more often than they suggested solutions. Their stinging indictments could be naively hopeful, at least to the extent that they anticipated benign answers to their prayers.

Though he was born a generation before the muckrakers, Bierce shared a similar religious and social background. He rebelled against that past, but he never entirely shook his Puritan antecedents. That struggle, blended with the lessons he had gleaned from his exposure to classical writing and a young life beset with more than the usual number of obstacles, shaped his dark view of the world and of mankind's natural capacity for reform. But those qualities also provided the raw material that helped create a muckraker, albeit an extremely ironic one.

NOTES

1. Ambrose Bierce, "Prattle," *San Francisco Examiner*, 26 May 1889, 4, as quoted in Lawrence I. Berkove, "Ambrose Bierce's Concern with Mind and Man" (Ph.D. dissertation, University of Pennsylvania, 1962), 94.

2. Janet M. Francendese, "Ambrose Bierce as Journalist" (Ph.D. dissertation, New York University, 1977), 202.

3. Walter Neale, *Life of Ambrose Bierce* (New York: Walter Neale, 1929), 228.

4. Ibid., 63.

5. Carey McWilliams, *Ambrose Bierce: A Biography* (New York: Albert & Charles Boni, 1929), 202.

6. Ibid., 169.

7. See, for example, H. L. Mencken, *A Mencken Chrestomathy* (New York: Alfred A. Knopf, 1949), 492–496.

8. "An Odd Preface," *Bookman*, 30 (October 1909), 125.

9. Henry Adams, *The Education of Henry Adams* (Boston: Houghton Mifflin Co., 1918), 240.

10. Fremont Older, *Growing Up* (San Francisco: San Francisco Call-Bulletin, 1931), 145.

11. Warren Theodore Francke, "Investigative Exposure in the Nineteenth Century: The Journalistic Heritage of the Muckrakers" (Ph.D. dissertation, University of Minnesota, 1974), 43–50.

12. Ibid., 1.

13. Ibid., 15–16.

14. Ibid., 17, 43–50.

15. Louis Filler, *The Muckrakers* (University Park: Pennsylvania State University Press, 1976), 415.

16. Ray Stannard Baker, *American Chronicle: The Autobiography of Ray Stannard Baker* (New York: Charles Scribner & Sons, 1945), 96.

17. Frank Luther Mott, *A History of American Magazines*, 4 vols. (Cambridge: Harvard University Press, 1957), 4:208.

18. Ibid., 4:209.

19. John Tebbel and Mary Ellen Zuckerman, *The Magazine in America: 1741–1990* (New York: Oxford University Press, 1991), 120.

20. Baker, 158, 183.

21. Filler, 111.

22. Ibid., 57.

23. Tebbel, 116.

24. David Mark Chalmers, *The Muckrake Years* (New York: D. Van Nostrand Co., 1974), 38.

25. Baker, 190.

26. Filler, 120.

27. David Graham Phillips, *The Treason of the Senate* (Stanford, Calif.: Academic Reprints, 1953), 104, as quoted in Barbara Cloud, "Muckraking Gets Its Name" (M.S. thesis, University of Oregon, 1967), 40.

28. Peter J. Frederick, *Knights of the Golden Rule: The Intellectual as Christian Social Reformer in the 1890s* (Lexington: University of Kentucky Press, 1976), 50, 110, 116.

29. Baker, 194.

30. George E. Mowry, *The California Progressives* (Berkeley: University of California Press, 1951), 88–89, 94–97; Chalmers, 69.

31. Richard E. Hofstadter, *The Age of Reform* (New York: Alfred A. Knopf, 1955), 136–138, 152, 186.

32. Cloud, 22.

33. Filler, 123.

34. Baker, 139.

35. Ida Tarbell, *All in the Day's Work* (Boston: G. K. Hall & Co., 1985), 399.

36. Ibid., 401.

37. Filler, 59.

38. Frederick, 304.

39. Baker, 133.

40. Ibid., 226.

41. Ibid., 183.

42. Francke, 74–77.

43. Ibid., 246, 256.

44. Francke, 325–327, 338; Filler, 26.

45. Francke, 181.

46. Ibid., 133.

47. Baker, 208–210.

48. Mott, 4:208; Francke, 224.

49. Filler, 115.

50. Francke, 14.

51. Baker, 93.

52. Filler, 31.

53. Ibid., 141.

54. Ibid., 133.

55. Ibid., 30.

56. Francke, 357.

57. Ibid., 82.

58. Filler, 414.

59. Baker, 180.

60. Chalmers, 25.

61. Filler, 416.

62. Baker, 32–33.

63. Francke, 173, 240.

64. Frederick, 11.

65. Tebbel, 114.

66. Baker, 202; Peterson, 448.

67. Baker, 195.

68. Tarbell, 400, 403.

69. Chalmers, 64–65.

70. Tebbel, 119.

71. Chalmers, 73.

72. Francke, 147.

73. Baker, 162.

74. Ibid., 184.

75. Charles Edward Russell, *Bare Hands and Stone Walls: Some Recoll-ections of a Side-Line Reformer* (New York: Charles Scribner's Sons, 1933).

76. Tebbel, 110.

4

The Journalist

BIOGRAPHICAL NOTES

A biographical sketch of Bierce helps explain his attitudes toward reform and his peculiar style of muckraking. His bitter resentment of his early family life, set off against the inspiring public life of his successful uncle, seems to have created a struggle within him. On one hand, he was, like his uncle, the crusader, pushing vocally and unyieldingly for often highly idiosyncratic types of reform. On the other, he was eternally revolting against the moral fervor of his ancestors and of his childhood. At the same time, a grounding in Stoicism absorbed from his father, his uncle, and others distinguished him from many later muckrakers.

He could not be portrayed as entirely naive, even as a youth. Almost from the beginning, he harbored serious reservations about the utility of his attacks. But these reservations grew and in themselves became strengths, providing him tremendous perseverance and a willingness to carry on an occasionally lonely battle against seemingly insurmountable odds.

Writers sometimes have attempted to categorize Bierce with a simple label, either as a "conservative" or as something of a "liberal," with racial, social, and economic attitudes to match the popular current usage of the particular term. Such labels are too easy. Limited enough in their descriptive powers now, they blur further when pushed back in history. The false assumption is that they meant the same thing a century ago that they do today. Applied to a shadowy, contradictory figure such as Bierce, they provide at best a kind of grotesque caricature rather than a reasonably clear facsimile of the writer's ideas.

Biographers often have highlighted the more colorful aspects of Bierce's life. Rather than concentrate on his influence or writing, they sometimes have chosen to dwell on his late-night perambulations through Northern California's foggy graveyards, his supposed trysts with female literary admirers, and his physical and verbal disputes with irate readers. Bierce's personal activities, or at least what biographers believe them to have been, can make stimulating reading, but conjuring them up seldom sheds much light on his ideas.

The influence of his activist uncle, Lucius V. Bierce, Ambrose's early introduction and repeated references as a mature writer to classical philosophy, especially that of the Stoics, and the change in his thought and expression that occurred during the forty years he wrote for newspapers and magazines all explain his journalism. But for the most part, these elements affecting his writing have been ignored or passed over lightly.

BACKGROUND AND EARLY LIFE

Bierce was born in Meigs County, Ohio, in June 1842, the last child of a farmer named Marcus Aurelius Bierce and his wife, Abigail, to survive into adulthood. His actual birthplace did not rate the status of a town. Horse Cave, Ohio, usually has been referred to as a "settlement." The place does not appear on maps today and apparently has returned to the dust whence it sprang. Some have suggested that he spent the better part of his life in cosmopolitan cities like London, New York, and San Francisco trying to shake the bonds of that remote childhood and to live down his bucolic past.

By the early 1800s, white settlers, including Bierce's parents, had reached that part of Ohio known as Connecticut's Western Reserve. Though standards had relaxed somewhat, the place was still in the grip of a Puritanism that had mellowed to a somewhat less rigid Presbyterianism.

In 1846, Ambrose, his parents, and his six brothers and sisters moved to Indiana, where his father continued to scratch out a living at farming. The family was poor, albeit in a somewhat genteel way. It was of old New England stock, and Marcus Aurelius Bierce kept a good library. This library appears, in fact, to have been the only positive attribute publicly granted him by his youngest son many years later.

Though Ambrose's father lived in obscurity, Ambrose's uncle Lucius Verus Bierce had carved a far different story out of his frontier life. Marcus Aurelius Bierce's younger brother had been named for the more obscure ruler who had shared power with the Roman emperor and Stoic philospher who was Marcus Aurelius Bierce's namesake. In the American version, it was Lucius Verus, not Marcus Aurelius, who was better remembered, and that influence appears to have made its mark on Ambrose.[1]

Lucius was an early graduate of Ohio University, then a frontier school. The college, situated in an American Athens far distant and different from its Hellenic namesake, had been established in 1812, four years before his matriculation. Though it occupied a two-room brick building, it had its aspirations. It was modeled on Yale University and its first de facto president and faculty member was a Princeton graduate and Presbyterian preacher who also grazed sheep on the side. In 1819, when Lucius was midway through his college career, the curriculum was heavily weighted with classics, including exercises in "Latin and Greek prosody" and the study of Cicero, Homer, and Tacitus, among others, along with a smattering of more contemporary courses with titles like "Moral Philosophy," "Metaphysics," and "Criticism of the best writers."[2] Besides indulging in such studies, Lucius took part in weekly debates of the Athenian Literary Society.

In 1822, shortly after graduating, Lucius embarked on a one-year, 1,800-mile walking tour of the South, recording his impressions in a journal that survives.[3] An early indication of the reform spirit that was to mark his adult life is registered in the shock and revolt with which he greeted a scene he encountered in Charleston, Virginia:

While here I saw, what, as it was my first sight of the Kind I had ever witnessed, was revolting to my feelings, and 'made me tremble to think that God was just.' It was the sight of an old Negro woman, probably forty or fifty years old, exposed, with her children, for sale, 'by virtue of an execution' from a court of Justice!! To see the cold indifference of the auctioneer and the sportive disregard of the spectators or purchasers as they examined her head, teeth, and eyes to discover her age; while the big tear rolling in silent agony down the cheek of the mother on viewing the prospects of a separation from her children, bespoke the anguish of the parent, and feelings more to be envied than those of her inhuman purchasers. I blushed that I was an American, and cursed the land that could thus traffic in human flesh.[4]

Upon his return to Ohio, Lucius undertook a distinguished if somewhat erratic career. He was given to political and social causes, sometimes hopeless ones, though hopelessness per se did not seem to deter his large energies. He became a lawyer and served as a prosecutor for

Portage County, where he combined integrity, a sense of the public welfare, ambition, and a supreme belief that he was in the right. Settling in Akron in 1828, he announced there was "not a decent man in it" and set about remedying the situation with his law practice and public spirit.

In 1838, Lucius Bierce, by that time a brigadier general at the head of a unit of Ohio militiamen called the Ravenna Invincibles, led a small, unauthorized, and misguided incursion into Canada. Lucius often had decried what he considered to be British tyranny. That year he sought to avenge some Canadian rebels who had fled to the United States following the failed Canadian Rebellion of 1837.

Bierce assembled 500 militiamen in Detroit. Only 137 actually accompanied him across the border into Windsor, where the little group was routed by 400 Canadian militiamen. Bierce escaped in a canoe down the Detroit River, but many of his men were either killed or captured. Some of the survivors eventually landed in a penal colony in Tasmania for violating the neutrality act governing relations between the United States and Canada.

In 1839, now honored as "the hero of Windsor" despite the debacle of his brief military campaign, Lucius was elected mayor of Akron. He served in that office for ten years, helping to establish the local public school system with the declaration that "the only hope of continuance of our government is the general diffusion of education and morality among the people."[5] Though he was an ardent embracer of causes—he was for sound money, temperance, good schools, streets, canals, and railroads, and strongly against slavery—he never remained loyal for long to one political party. None seemed equal to his ideals. Ambitious, strong-willed, and always sure of the justice of whatever movement he happened to be championing, he lacked the political ability for compromise.

He helped found a newspaper called the *Democratic Standard* but abandoned it in 1852 when it refused to print his anti-slavery writings. That same year he ran for Congress as an independent and lost. In 1855, he helped supply the radical abolitionist John Brown with arms on his way to fight slavery in the Kansas Territory. (Like Bierce—and Collis P. Huntington—Brown had been born in Litchfield County, Connecticut.) When Brown was hanged four years later after the Harper's Ferry raid, Bierce eulogized him before a crowd in Akron.

As Lucius Bierce grew older, he drifted away from politics and from the Presbyterianism of his earlier years. Both "idealistic and restless," he became, in the words of one writer, "the embodiment of the spirit of the Western Reserve: the Puritan conscience set free from the restraint of dogma, emphasizing the freedom and dignity of the individual."[6]

Lucius clearly influenced his young nephew Ambrose. To a boy stuck on a poor, backward farm and yearning for escape, his uncle's exploits must have seemed a marvelous and bright, shining light pointing the way out from a miserable obscurity.

Later in life, Ambrose probably tempered his youthful idolization of his uncle with irony. Lucius's penchant for failed causes, and the curiously favorable reactions of his fellow townsfolk, perhaps contributed to Ambrose's irony and skepticism. One of Bierce's more humorous and biting short stories, "Jupiter Doke: Brigadier General," is redolent of Lucius's absurd military exploits. It tells the tale of a bungling, pompous Union brigadier general from the Midwest who wins a victory not by strategy or tactics but by inadvertently stampeding a herd of mules. The unskilled but lucky general nevertheless is universally lauded, receiving plaudits in the newspapers and decorations from the military brass. Only the most insignificant character in the story, a black teamster, understands the truth. Naturally, everyone ignores him.[7]

EDUCATION

Young Ambrose's only formal "high" education came courtesy of his locally famous uncle. In 1859, Lucius arranged for his seventeen-year-old nephew to attend the Kentucky Military Institute, then "one of the highest class institutions of its kind in the country." It is unclear exactly how long Ambrose attended the school, although it appears he stayed there for less than a year.[8] He also worked at an anti-slavery Indiana newspaper as a printer's devil, an occupation which in the nineteenth century served to train many aspiring newspaper writers and editors.

Bierce acquired most of his education on his own. Francendese and Berkove have pointed out that his critics and biographers have largely ignored his classicism, which undoubtedly had a large influence on his outlook and writing. The fact that his father and uncle were named for Roman emperors should be an obvious clue to this inclination, as should the heavy dose of classics administered to Bierce's esteemed uncle while a student at Ohio University.

His uncle and father's examples were reinforced later by James Watkins, a newspaperman and Bierce's editor at the *San Francisco News-Letter*. As an early mentor of Bierce, the English expatriate urged the young writer to study the classics (along with a liberal helping of English and French satire by writers such as Swift and La Rochefoucauld) in his early days in San Francisco. Throughout his career, Bierce sprinkled his newspaper writings with classical allusions, especially to the Stoics Epictetus and Marcus Aurelius, themselves heavily influenced by the Cynic tradition. Their outlook was essentially cyclical and fatalistic. Human history for them was what one scholar has termed "endless change, yet wearisome monotony."[9]

Unlike the popular understanding of cynicism extant today as well as in Bierce's time, this outlook did not suggest either a retreat from public life or the public recitation of pious lies as a way of camouflaging one's baser motives and getting ahead in the world. The militant branch of the early Greek Cynics practiced a kind of "radical Stoicism" and were men with a mission who sought to spread the truth as they understood it. Like Diogenes, they took upon themselves the job of "criticizing conventional values [and] exposing shams," and they "were unimpressed by reputation of any kind."[10] For Epictetus, the true Cynic "must know that he is sent as a messenger from God to men concerning things good and evil, to show them that they have gone astray and are seeking the true nature of good and evil where it is not to be found, and take no thought where it really is."[11]

In a land newly populated by white settlers, such thought did not necessarily contradict the frontier spirit. It fostered a respect for the individual and self-sufficiency combined with a frequent contempt for law, authority, and what passed for learning and culture. It had parallels with Puritanism as well. It commended self-denial and abstinence from pleasure. Many of its restrictions and ideals, like those of Puritanism, would be next to impossible for any mortal to carry out faithfully. Epictetus, in "The Calling of a Cynic," cautions aspirants: "You must harbor no anger, wrath, envy, pity: a fair maid, a fair name, favorites, or sweet cakes, must mean nothing to you."[12]

To convey their message, the Cynics favored aphorisms. Pithy sayings were easily memorized and digested by their audiences. The style ideally suited Bierce and his journalism; practically all of his writing is terse and compact, and its literary quality often varies inversely with its length, as with his aphoristic *Devil's Dictionary*.

THE CIVIL WAR

Soon after the Civil War began, Ambrose enlisted as a private in an Indiana regiment. His reasons for enlisting are obscure, although probably the lure of war for many young men—the possibility of glory and the certainty of escaping the petty cares of civilian life—played a part. Ambrose had worked at a couple of demeaning jobs in Elkhart, Indiana, as a brickyard worker and as a kind of waiter, and probably he hoped to escape the sheer drudgery of that sort of labor. Some urge for reform may have guided him to war, especially considering his uncle's views and the fact that Ambrose himself had worked for an anti-slavery newspaper. His sometimes unreliable publisher Neale claims Bierce "fought to liberate the slaves."[13]

Bierce served with distinction, rising to the rank of lieutenant (and breveted to major after the war). The conflict clearly changed him. Perhaps it smashed some of his youthful illusions, or merely reinforced an innate suspicion of the stupidity and viciousness of men. In 1912, shortly before he disappeared, he revisited some of the battlefields of his youth—Chickamauga, Shiloh, Nashville, Kennesaw Mountain, among others. One photograph from the time shows him clad in black and wearing a mournful expression. His recollections of the war in his *Works* often carry an elegiac, even sentimental, tone.

A severe head wound Bierce suffered at the Battle of Kennesaw Mountain in Georgia in 1864 gave some who knew him, including certain members of the Bierce family, the impression that the war had taken both a physical and emotional toll. He became a much more difficult and bitter person after he was wounded, a brother claimed. Occasionally it was implied that he was not quite rational, and up to his disappearance, and even after, he was occasionally suspected of insanity.

Others have described the change as simply spiritual. The carnage that Bierce had endured in war, the stupidity, the violence, the chaos, made him lash out at human weakness, viciousness, and deceit when he reentered civilian life. War also taught him that a broad gulf often separated theory and reality—that the neat and ideal political theories of freeing the slaves and preserving the Union uttered by politicians were at some remove from the ugly realities of maiming and killing and plundering—and added to the skeptical view of human nature that he already had begun to cultivate on his father's dank farm.[14]

He returned to his parents' home only twice after enlisting, once to recover from his head wound and again for a visit shortly after the war's end. Many years later, he supposedly described his family to a friend, the poet George Sterling, as "unwashed savages."[15] For the rest of his life, apparently, Bierce kept in contact only with one brother, Albert, who had moved to Oakland, California. His siblings never gained the notoriety he earned as a writer, though the Bierce penchant to edify and startle the public did manifest itself in other ways: a sister became a missionary in Africa and a brother wound up as a circus strongman.

BIERCE IN THE WEST: JOURNALISM AND ITS DISCONTENTS

Bierce's disillusion with the war, a period he later recalled as both exhilarating and horrifying, was followed by government service as a United States Treasury Department agent in Reconstruction Alabama, where corruption was rampant. Then, under his former Civil War commander, William B. Hazen, he helped scout the West for the United States Army. In 1867, he resigned from the expedition after it reached San Francisco.

His earliest writing there consisted of atheistic tracts and "wild denunciations of all religions."[16] As early as 1867, he was contributing poems and sketches to the *Californian*, at a time when a backlash against the booster journalism that had been so prevalent in the Golden State the previous decade was taking hold. The tall tales of Western heroes, praise of California's supposedly perfect climate, breathless accounts of the social events of the day, and paeans to businesses of all types gave way to satire of the same. To a man of Bierce's mind, the distended puffery of the booster press offered a wide and inviting target. He was continuing to attack newspapers' slavish backslapping in 1870:

Can anybody do anything in San Francisco without deserving great credit for it? A fire occurs and the firemen exterminate it, as they are paid to do. They deserve great credit, says the Daily Beslaverum. A thief is arrested for a crime, having committed a dozen with impunity. Officer Layfrim deserves great credit for having accepted his surrender. Manager Muckrake bilks the public with a new show. He deserves great credit for the admirable manner in which it is put on the stage, ejaculates the Morning Soapumdown. . . . There are probably a few intelligent persons in this city who have been driven by fate to do reporting—we personally know one or two—but the majority of them have not sufficient sense to coldly furnish forth an intellectual feast for a dyspeptic idiot. They know how to dose anybody and everybody who will tolerate them an instant, with praise that would turn the stomach of a moral ostrich, but they don't know anything else. . . . We 'deserve great credit' for not burning them at sight—the feeble-witted, fat-headed parasites![17]

Such was Bierce's early view of journalism, at least as commonly practiced, and his opinion of the craft did not improve during the rest of his career. Journalism was many things to Bierce, but primarily it was a way to make a living—and not a bad one, despite the contentions of de Castro that Bierce was financially hard pressed.

Bierce did endure financial uncertainty between jobs, but he started on the *Examiner* in 1887 at $75 a week, a salary that eventually was increased by a third. There were journalists at the turn of the century who made more money—during the Spanish-American War, well-known writers like Stephen Crane and Frank Norris commanded as much as $3,000 a month—but the typical reporter made much less. The muck-raker David Graham Phillips, for instance, started as a cub reporter on the *Cincinnati Star* at ten dollars a week in 1887 and was getting fifteen dollars a week three years later after he moved to the *New York Sun*.[18] A "comfortable" yearly income for magazine writers in 1885 was $2,000.[19] Bierce's pay was not a trifling sum, particularly in an age racked by frequent economic depressions, when a steak dinner cost twenty-five cents and an apprentice in Huntington's shipyard in Newport News could expect to take home eight dollars a week.

Nevertheless, Bierce's view of his occupation was mixed, and it soured with experience. He in fact attempted escape in the Black Hills of Dakota in 1880, when he sought his fortune with a mining company there. Undercapitalized and ineptly managed, however, the company failed despite Bierce's best efforts, and he had to return to journalism.[20]

Although he looked down on many of his colleagues in the press, most of whom he considered little more than fools, sycophants, or worse, he appeared to have some hope, at least early in his career, of reforming the trade. His words sometimes made it sound as if he planned an almost holy enterprise. In his inaugural column of "Prattle" in the *Argonaut* in 1877, he gravely warned: "It is my intention to purify journalism in this town by instructing such writers as it is worth while to instruct, and assaulting those that it is not."[21] Five years later, he still held out hope for journalism as something more than mere sustenance for hacks. "The end which a journalist should have in view," he wrote early in his career on the *Wasp*, "is the dignity and purity and wisdom of his journal—the elevation of his profession."[22]

Yet his belief in the improvability of man and journalist, not strong even in his early years, can be overstated. Once he defined newspapers as "conducted by rogues and dunces for dunces and rogues. . . . They fetter the feet of wisdom and stiffen the prejudices of the ignorant. They are sycophants to the mob, tyrants to the individual."[23] His view of journalism as practiced in the wide-open town of San Francisco was especially disdainful: "In other places journalists are disingenuous. Here they are liars from principle." Through their lies, ignorance, and servility, journalists "invited and directed" the counterattacks of each adversary. They devalued themselves professionally, in effect selling their birthright for a mess of pottage. For Bierce, "to despise my enemy and make him respect me—that is the whole battle."[24] To win that contest, he considered it essential to maintain the moral high ground.

Though he took upon himself the role of scourge of these multitudes of liars and sycophants, maneuvering to get in his sights any false persons, especially those in positions of power, he usually refrained from allying himself with any of their traditional foes. He loved neither democracy nor the hoi polloi. "The masses"—he was always careful to distance himself from the term with sardonic quotation marks—were assumed to be honest and intelligent. They were neither, and this false assumption was an "inherent weakness" of democracy.[25] The "wild ass of public opinion" was fickle, ignorant, and ultimately worthless, yet "no European court journal, no European courtier, was ever more abject in subservience to the sovereign than are the American newspaper and the American politician in flattery of the people."[26]

Bierce's disdain for journalism is unlikely to have resulted from any sense of personal failure in its practice. Though he did not really attain any lasting national fame, especially as a journalist, his appointment by Hearst as columnist for the *Examiner* made him for a time a regional and even occasionally a national eminence. For most of his career with Hearst, Bierce saw his weekly column appear prominently on the editorial page. He became a leading literary, cultural, and social critic in the West. Many of his contemporaries even blamed his satirical thrusts for the suicide of a little-known San Francisco poet named David Lezinsky and later for the assassination of President William McKinley by the fanatical anarchist Leon Csolgosz. Though the charges are almost certainly false, they give some measure of the perceived power of his pen at the time.

But for Bierce, eminence in journalism was a shabby honor. Societies, he wrote, endured through their art and through nothing else: "the Spartans are remembered today only because of the things the artistic Athenians wrote about them." Americans' preoccupation with "possessing things and being in turn possessed by them" would doom them to a place in history alongside the Spartans rather than the Athenians.[27]

Was it art—journalism, that is? For Bierce, it was not. Whether he was being disingenuous, or whether this pronouncement was an example of his own inability to understand himself, it remains true that some of his best writing, his fictional war tales, drew much of their power from the elements of good journalism: observation, experience, understanding, clarity, precision, and simplicity of language. The bulk of his short stories were also journalism in another sense. They originally appeared in the same newspapers and magazines that contained his columns and they owed much of their style to the rigors and constraints of newspaper writing.

Yet Bierce abhorred realism. He reviled the realistic school of fiction advanced by writers like William Dean Howells and maintained that "genius . . . is the faculty of knowing things without having to learn them."[28] The true artist had to lift his sights from the streets to the heavens. Bierce's advice to one pupil, the poet Herman Scheffauer, was typical of his approach to art: "Do not write about ignoble persons."[29] The bulk of his newspaper journalism was devoted, in fact, to flaying ignoble persons of various stripes. Perhaps it was in the supposedly ideal world of art that he sought refuge. He never confused his journalism with art.

Bierce's own attempts at what he considered to be the highest form of art—poetry—often seem clumsy, threadbare, or overwrought. Jerome Hart, a colleague during Bierce's early days on the Argonaut, pointed out to him the failings of one of his poems one day. "You are right," Bierce is said to have replied. "Hart, let me tell you something. When I was in my twenties, I concluded one day that I was not a poet. *It was the bitterest moment of my life.*"[30]

Hart ridiculed Bierce—Bierce had railed against Hart many times in his columns, turning him into one of his numerous enemies—for misidentifying an anonymous poem as a classic, only to be informed by a reader that it was actually a fragment of tripe from a *McGuffey's Reader* for schoolchildren. A similar story is told of Bierce, Mark Twain, and English friends at leisure in London. Bierce is asked to read a passage in a book containing several languages and is unable to understand or even properly pronounce the foreign passages, although he sometimes trotted out foreign phrases in his columns. The scene is frequently cited as one of terrible embarrassment for Bierce and amusement for his colleagues. It is meant to portray Bierce not only as a faker, but as a man pathetically unable to escape the fetters of his humble beginnings.[31]

BIERCE, REFORM, AND REFORMERS

Though Bierce attacked many powerful persons and institutions, he seemed to have little or no sympathy for other journalists who made such attacks or for other persons who today might be called "activists." He turned on one of his pupils, Edwin Markham, when Markham, then a teacher, wrote and published "The Man with the Hoe," a poem that took up the cudgels for the plight of the workingman. The poem became incredibly popular and advanced the writing career of Markham, who himself later dabbled in muckraking.

For Bierce, feminists were at best "femininnies," their male supporters "he-hens."[32] Hearst, ever sensitive to circulation, for a time tried to balance Bierce's attacks on the feminists' cause by inserting columns under the byline of suffragette Susan B. Anthony adjacent to Bierce's "Prattle."

Though Berkove has asserted that Bierce "repeatedly defended such social pariahs as Chinese, Mormons, and Jews from the rampant bigots of the town [San Francisco]," Bierce, though hardly a bigot, was no crusading reformer on the issues of race and religion. Francendese's assessment of Bierce's attitude as "ambivalent" is probably more accurate. His support of a particular group usually rested less upon his sympathy for it than upon his antipathy to the group that was making the attack. For instance, it was not so much that he supported Chinese immigrants to San Francisco, whom he occasionally ridiculed but just as often defended. His hatred of Denis Kearney and his Workingmen's Party often prompted his defense of the Chinese. Kearney's group, composed mostly of Irish immigrants, began harassing the Chinese during the economic depression of the 1870s.[33]

Bierce's thought on class was just as ambivalent. Though he occasionally expressed concern about the plight of the poor, he averred that the problem of poverty could not be solved, though its conditions might be ameliorated. In this as in other things, he was fond of quoting Scripture (odd practice indeed for a journalist who once had written atheistic screeds): "The poor always ye have with you." To Bierce, sentiments such as those contained in Markham's poem merely served to whip up class hatred "while preaching the benefits of brotherhood."[34]

At various times, Bierce advocated a progressive income tax, the abolishment of private ownership of land, an end to the import of cheap labor, and an early form of "workfare" in which every citizen would be guaranteed a job, albeit one at low wages. He never advocated socialism, although he once loosely characterized himself as "something of a socialist," and one biographer has categorized him as "a more earnest reformer—even humanitarian—than he admitted or knew."[35] Still, he seemed to have little faith that reform measures would solve any of the world's ancient problems. The fundamental flaw lay in human nature: "The world does not wish to be helped. The poor wish only to be rich, which is impossible, not to be better. They would like to be rich in order to be worse, generally speaking."[36]

Wealth rather than "betterment" was also ignoble—a conclusion not far from Cynical and Stoical reasoning. On the other hand, Bierce harbored no romantic illusions about the poverty from which he himself had escaped. He was, like Phillips, a natural aristocrat, and he lived comfortably. In personal matters, he tended to grant wealth its social perquisites. In one letter to a lawyer for the mining company he represented in the Black Hills, he contrasted a "gentleman, wealthy and influential" with an "impecunious fellow, commonly found in bar-rooms, [with] no social standing."[37]

He was at best uneasy about the sorts of reform programs that his uncle Lucius could have embraced wholeheartedly and that have repeatedly swept across the United States. In one column, he doubted the benefits of universal college education, pointing out that there would not be a sufficient number of worthwhile jobs for graduates. They would, he predicted, be less inclined to do menial but necessary tasks and become dissatisfied when forced to assume such drudgery in order to eat.[38]

Howells's fantastic Altruria and all utopian communities, fictional or real, were doomed to failure because they were based on the false premise that "social ills are accidental rather than essential consequences of human nature."[39] Reform ultimately was unworkable because it absolved humans of individual responsibility and rendered society's institutions, faulty as they were, impotent. For Bierce, it often came down to responsibility: "Who can 'lash the rascals naked through the world' in an age that holds crime to be a disease, and converts the prisons into a sanitarium?"[40]

The California Progressives were largely repugnant to him, though they put strict limits on the railroad corruption that he had exposed for much of his career. In 1910, a decade after Bierce had left California, a Progressive governor, Hiram Johnson, was elected, and a reform-minded legislature was installed soon after. But Bierce had little sympathy for their aims. In a November 1911 letter to his friend Sterling, he observed: "I note that at the late election California damned herself to a still lower degradation and is now unfit for a white man to live in. Initiative, referendum, recall, employer's liability, woman suffrage—yah!'"[41]

Like other midwesterners, including many of the generation of muckrakers that followed him, Bierce had been imbued with Protestant habits of hard work, ambition, and a respect for study. He had been born in a decade that fostered what one historian has characterized as "the most fervent and diverse outburst of reform energy in American history."[42] He managed to distance himself from the stern and gloomy Puritanism that smothered him during his youth, but he never completely escaped it.

Theology and reform had been closely linked in America in the 1840s. Hell-fire revivals formed the religious side of the civic push for social change. Reform became a kind of secular branch of Protestantism; Protestantism and Puritanism had themselves grown out of religious reform. Perhaps religion and reform were never entirely separated in Bierce's mind. Certainly, he lashed out at both. But in so doing, he became a reformer of reformers, a purifier of Puritans.

The old Calvinist notion of a soul seeking salvation from inherent sinfulness along the tricky path of predestination was being replaced by beliefs in improvement and prosperity. Reform, according to one thesis, was a way of coping with the technological changes of the nineteenth century, a way of adapting the ancient verities of moral rigor to the modern age of steampower, corrupt politics, and big money.[43]

Bierce never made the adjustment. He saw little hope for improvement beyond the occasional remarkable individual. No matter how he "lashed the rascals," no matter how many screeds he fired off against the pious frauds of the day, their supply seemed inexhaustible. Yet amid the epicurean pleasures of California, he could never quite live up to the impossible demands set by a Stoicism he fashioned out of an innate Puritanism. Some writers have attributed his supposed immunity to the "disease" of "reformitis" to his Puritan roots, but this is likely only insofar as he considered most reformers as damned as anyone else.[44]

His personal standards regarding earthly temptations could border on prissiness. On a canoe trip, he is reported to have threatened to shoot Sterling, clad in a bathing suit, unless he jumped overboard, thereby sparing Ambrose's niece Laura Bierce and Sterling's wife the trauma of viewing Sterling in his swimming apparel.[45] Bierce left his wife after discovering a love letter from another man.[46]

Bierce in another sense was the apotheosis of the Horatio Alger success ideal popular during the nineteenth century. He rose from obscure and poor origins on a frontier farm to attain a measure of fame. But his life at the same time was an ironical answer to such popular rags-to-riches tales, a kind of tragicomic burlesque of the Alger story with the happy ending. It was a life of deepening disillusion, both personal and professional. His two sons died while they were young men. His fiction never got the acclaim he thought it deserved. At the end of his career in journalism, he was treated not as a kind of elder statesman, but as a sort of old-fashioned crank. The editors of *Cosmopolitan*, much younger men than Bierce and much less experienced, rejected or attempted to alter many of his submissions and seemed interested only in his worst material.

He had been born to failure, as one writer has pointed out. The movement west of his parents' generation had been a disappointment. The advantages of the rich midwestern loam over the New England hardscrabble had not rescued Bierce's parents and many other emigrants from the economic vagaries of farming. Like other writers of his generation, Bierce was "less a product of the movement West" than of "the movement's failed dreams."[47]

In response, Bierce set about laying down an enfilade of verbal fire on virtually all ranks of society. The reports carried, though softly, into the next century. For Mencken, "there was no more discretion in Bierce than you will find in a runaway locomotive. . . . He was the first American to lay about him with complete gusto, charging and battering the frauds who ranged the country."[48] The metaphor is curiously appropriate, given Bierce's struggle with the railroad, and it is possible that Mencken, as a youth in Baltimore, had noticed Bierce's duel with Huntington in Washington.

In the end, Bierce's lifetime of revolt against the fraudulent dream was not enough. Shortly before he disappeared, he wrote in a despairing letter to his daughter, Helen: "In America, you can't go East or West any more, or North, the only avenue of escape is South."[49] His background had fit him to be a reluctant muckraker, seeking to spread salvation but at the same time doubting the likelihood of achieving that goal. He confirmed these suspicions during his long career in journalism. But the example of the Stoics suggested that although the fight was always futile in the long run, it was worth doing for itself. If Bierce lacked some of the inherent optimism of the muckrakers, he also did not share wholly in their naive belief that exposing a problem meant solving it.

He held in common the muckrakers' typical religious background. But in his case, that upbringing provoked as much distaste as moral certainty. Then, too, there was the war. Men like Baker had marched with Coxey's Army—an army of the poor and jobless that Jacob Coxey had led in a futile protest to Washington, D.C., in 1894. Bierce had marched with the Union Army. Both journalists had witnessed the collision of enlightened notions with brute force, but Bierce had seen it on a much larger and more chaotic scale, and as a participant as well as an observer. The war and its aftermath could not have helped but temper his enthusiasm for putting ideals into action.

NOTES

1. Carey McWilliams, *Ambrose Bierce: A Biography* (New York: Albert & Charles Boni, 1929), 24; Adolphe de Castro, *Portrait of Ambrose Bierce* (New York: The Century Co.), 4.

2. Edwin W. Smith, *The Life and Times of Daniel Lindley: 1801–1880.* (London: The Epworth Press, 1949), 18–23.

3. Lucius Verus Bierce, *Travels in the Southland, 1822–1823: The Journal of Lucius Verus Bierce, with a Biographical Essay by George W. Knepper* (Columbus: Ohio State University Press, 1966).

4. Ibid., 53–54.

5. Knepper, biographical essay in *Lucius Bierce*, 20–21.

6. Ibid., 31, 38.

7. Morris traces the story to a Confederate nighttime attack in 1863 near Lookout Mountain, Tennessee. After mules were set free by Union teamsters, the Rebel attackers became convinced they were under cavalry assault and fled. Morris does not mention Bierce's uncle, but it is likely that Bierce also derived his short story from from his own experiences; the piece includes "Horsecave" in the series of backwaters visited by the hapless Doke. Roy Morris, Jr., *Ambrose Bierce: Alone in Bad Company* (New York: Crown Publishers, 1995), 67–70.

8. McWilliams, 25.

9. Charles Bigg, introduction to *The Meditations of Marcus Aurelius* (London: Oxford at the Clarendon Press, 1906), 37.

10. Donald R. Dudley, *A History of Cynicism* (London: Methuen & Co., 1937), 37, 199.

11. Whitney J. Oates, ed. *The Stoic and Epicurean Philosophers: The Complete Extant Writings of Epicurus, Epictetus, Lucretius, and Marcus Aurelius* (New York: Random House, 1940), 378.

12. Ibid., 377.

13. Walter Neale, *Life of Ambrose Bierce* (New York: Walter & Neale, 1929), 194.

14. Lawrence I. Berkove, "The Man with the Burning Pen" *Journal of Popular Culture*, 15 (1981), 34–38; McWilliams, 233.

15. McWilliams, 21–23.

16. Ibid., 81.

17. As quoted in Jerome Hopkins, ed., *The Ambrose Bierce Satanic Reader* (New York: Doubleday & Co., 1968), 76.

18. Barbara Cloud, "Muckraking Gets Its Name" (M.S. thesis, University of Oregon, 1967), 6–8.

19. John Tebbel and Mary Ellen Zuckerman, *The Magazine in America: 1741–1990* (New York: Oxford University Press, 1991), 61.

20. Paul Fatout, *Ambrose Bierce and the Black Hills* (Norman: University of Oklahoma Press, 1956), 45.

21. Frank Luther Mott, *A History of American Magazines*, 4 vols. (Cambridge: Harvard University Press, 1957), 3:57.

22. *Wasp*, 23 September 1882, as quoted in Janet M. Francendese, "Ambrose Bierce as Journalist" (Ph.D. dissertation, New York University, 1977), 18.

23. McWilliams, 168.

24. Hopkins, *Satanic Reader*, 88.

25. Ambrose Bierce, *The Collected Works of Ambrose Bierce* (New York: The Neale Publishing Co., 1909–1912), 1:61.

26. Ibid., 11:302, 344.

27. Neale, 73.

28. Bierce, *Works*, 10:288.

29. Joseph Noel, *Footloose in Arcadia* (New York: Carrick & Evans, 1940), 325.

30. Jerome Hart, *In Our Second Century* (San Francisco: The Pioneer Press, 1931), 153. The italics are Hart's.

31. Neale, 42.

32. Bierce, *Works*, 10:146.

33. Berkove, *Popular Culture*, 35; Francendese, 136.

34. Francendese, 85.

35. Paul Fatout, *Ambrose Bierce: The Devil's Lexicographer* (Norman: University of Oklahoma Press, 1951), 207–208.

36. Van Wyck Brooks, *Emerson and Others* (New York: E. P. Dutton & Co., 1927), 153.

37. Fatout, *Black Hills*, 136.

38. "Prattle," 15 July 1894, as quoted in Francendese, 148.

39. Francendese, 110–111.

40. Bierce, *Works*, 10:282.

41. C. Hartley Grattan, *Bitter Bierce: A Mystery of American Letters* (New York: Doubleday & Co., 1929), 231.

42. Ronald G. Walters, *American Reformers: 1815-1860* (New York: Hill & Wang, 1978), ix.

43. Ibid., 23, 214.

44. Neale, 67.

45. Noel, 200.

46. Franklin Walker, *Ambrose Bierce: The Wickedest Man in San Francisco* (San Francisco: The Colt Press, 1941), 35.

47. David G. Anderson, in Kathy N. Davidson, *Critical Essays on Ambrose Bierce* (Boston: G. K. Hall & Co., 1982), 97–98.

48. H. L. Mencken, *A Mencken Chrestomathy* (New York: Alfred A. Knopf, 1949), 496.

49. McWilliams, 316.

5

The Railroad

Collis P. Huntington made an admirable arch-villain for Bierce's muck-raking. Burly and bewhiskered, Huntington offered the journalist a wide and slow-moving target. The man in real life was almost a caricature of the robber baron of the time—grossly overweight, smugly self-assured in his selfishness, and given to placidly feeding trite snippets of folk wisdom to a fawning press while at the same time jealously guarding each quarter in his multimillion-dollar empire and buying and selling politicians and journalists like so many barrels of pork.

Railroads in reality differed starkly from how they typically were portrayed. They had been sold to California's populace and to the rest of the country by railroad writers as well as by various businessmen, reformers, and others. Some had advocated them purely for personal profit and some had harbored broader motives. Bierce's uncle Lucius had included construction of railroads in his panoply of good works for Ohio. Promises of open markets, universal prosperity, and a more civilized life were kept, to varying degrees, but were delivered along with greed, corruption, and monopoly. In California, a kept press labored to keep the illusion intact by ignoring the railroad's ignominies and concentrating on its benefits to the local economy.

HUNTINGTON

If Bierce was a kind of Horatio Alger story recited in front of a funhouse mirror, Huntington, the sly, avaricious leader of the Big Four, appeared as its more straightforward reflection in a form that many Americans could respect and understand if not necessarily love. The appearance, however, had to be contrived with certain gaps masking some of Huntington's more unsavory means to fortunate ends.

Though they jousted in the public arena, Bierce and Huntington shared similar backgrounds and even some attitudes. Like Bierce, Huntington despised Markham and his "hoe poem." Queried about it by a reporter for the New York Sun, Huntington objected: "Is America going to turn to socialism over one poem? Markham's man has a hoe. Let him rejoice. The only man to commiserate is the man who has no hoe; the man who can't help to enrich the world."[1] Always a man of action, Huntington went so far as to offer $700 through a newspaper for the best poem refuting Markham's sentiments in a new poem to be titled "The Man without the Hoe." The contest attracted some five thousand entries.

Huntington's family, like Bierce's and John Brown's, had its roots in Litchfield County, Connecticut. Like Bierce, Huntington exhibited some Puritanical traits, including a devotion to hard work and occupation and a personal prohibition against certain perceived vices. For Huntington, this distaste manifested itself in an abstention from drinking and smoking that endured past middle age.

The railroad man never shared the reform instincts of men like John Brown and Lucius Bierce, though he did come down on the reform side of the racial divide, taking a stance against slavery. He supported the Free Soilers as a young man in California and later took a moderate stance in helping blacks help themselves with contributions to Booker T. Washington's Tuskegee Institute. But overall, Huntington was apt to regard reformers with suspicion. In the words of one historian, "there is no record that he ever wanted to reform anything, or, except where personal interest was involved, to change anything." Like Bierce, he was proudly individualistic and believed that such change as could be effected was largely accomplished through personal effort.[2]

The railroad magnate was almost a textbook Alger character, pulling himself up from an obscure and difficult boyhood—if one ignored the methods he used to propel himself. Born in 1821, Huntington grew up in a section of Harwinton, Connecticut, known as "Poverty Hollow." Many years later, when he became famous, newspapers often repeated this name as an integral part of the rags-to-riches litany, especially in the many favorable obituaries that followed his demise.

Like Bierce, he came from a family whose size was in inverse proportion to its wealth. His father had been a tinker, and his mother overburdened with children. Circumstances became so severe that Collis often stayed with other families as a child. Some biographers later attributed his success to his humble beginnings.[3] But along with Bierce, Huntington's origins were terribly but for that time not extraordinarily poor. It did not go unnoticed that the later fight against the railroad barons was, in one sense, "the spectacle of the plain people attacking themselves." Many of these successful capitalists were but one remove from the small towns and farms that now harbored enemies who complained of unfair freight rates and political corruption.[4]

Huntington was a strong, rough boy whose principal scholastic achievement seemed to consist of having thrashed two of his teachers. One had made the mistake of trying to correct Huntington's poor spelling by striking him a heavy blow on the hand with a stick each time his pupil made an error. The corporal method proved unsound. Huntington remained a poor speller throughout his life, an impediment that did not seem to do him much temporal harm despite his beaten schoolmaster's disapproval.

At fourteen, Huntington left home to work as an itinerant merchant in upstate New York. He continued to toil in the East until 1849, when he struck out for California and its Gold Rush. Never really intending to slave away as a miner, he actually hefted a shovel for less than a day. Like the other members of the Big Four, he was shrewd enough even as a young man to realize that the chances of extracting money from the gold diggers were greater than those of extracting gold from the diggings. Selling shovels, rather than digging with them, was a surer path to riches.

He made plenty of money as a merchant, though he did not become fantastically rich until he got into railroading. On his way to California down the Atlantic coast, across Central America, and back up the Pacific coast, he managed to quadruple his initial capital of $1,200 through various retail enterprises with his fellow travelers. Later as a merchant in California, he won a small fortune by cornering the market in shovels—a mundane but nevertheless very necessary item during a gold rush.

It was perhaps his first lesson in the successful manipulation of public opinion. Having laid in all available shovels, driving the price from $2.50 to $125 a dozen, he publicized the latter, extraordinary figure. Rather than quieting demand, news of this outlandish price triggered a buying panic. Huntington was soon selling shovels at $240 a dozen. He later established as a general business theory that if a buyer protested loudly but still paid the asking price, the seller was charging all that the market could bear and therefore obeying the basic law of laissez-faire capitalism.

Eventually, Huntington went into business with Mark Hopkins in Sacramento, opening a dry-goods store. Huntington eschewed perishable items in his inventory, wishing only to deal in things that he could hold indefinitely until he got his price. Not only was he a tough seller, but he kept a sharp eye on personal as well as business expenses. After he had become a multimillionaire, his remark to a hotel clerk discovered to have overcharged him by a quarter became almost legendary in San Francisco: "Young man, you can't follow me through life by the quarters I have dropped."[5]

RAILROADS AS SYMBOLS OF HOPE AND PROGRESS

Railroads had been boosted by special "railroad writers" for nearly four decades by the time the transcontinental link was complete. These boosters included editors, essayists, book reviewers, and even poets, who began their work in 1827 singing the praises of construction of the first public railroad in the United States, from Baltimore to Ohio.

Economic advancement lay at the core of their arguments, though they promised a young nation much more. Smoke-belching steam engines would "secure the nation's defense, . . . cure poverty, ignorance, and promote health." Railroads would put America on a more nearly equal footing with cultured Europe and "could only uplift the country's moral character and raise its level of civilization." Railroad boosters, who labored mightily at their task until the Civil War, did not forget the vast and deserted West. In 1853, a writer in *Putnam's Monthly Magazine* promised readers that a western railroad would surpass "the Pyramids of Egypt, the great Roman Military Roads, the Simplon of Napoleon." Many of the articles had about them a "kind of desperate energy" intimating that the roads were the last best hope to hold the young United States together. Railroads could be all things to all people, serving both individual needs and the public good.[6]

The idea of financing railroads with the abundant and vacant public lands in the West became popular during a severe shortage of capital in the 1840s. Boosters meanwhile emphasized the benefits to the public that would accrue from financing the roads with public funds. They suggested that the projects would open markets, stimulate the economy, and narrow the gap between rich and poor by providing a universal prosperity.

The symbolism of nineteenth-century railroads in America can be overdone, as perhaps occurred when one historian likened the "pure white jet" of locomotives' steam to a "mechanistic orgasm" indicative of nineteenth-century repression of women, blacks, Mexicans, Asians, and Native Americans, among others.[7] With apologies to Dr. Freud, one must point out that there are times when a locomotive is just a locomotive. Nevertheless, the railroad was a powerful political and economic symbol, and a hopeful one, and it was used as such by the press.

Boosters played to Americans' optimism, assuring them that railroads would open up the riches of the West to all, and Americans seemed to embrace the idea. After the groundbreaking for the Baltimore & Ohio in 1828, railroad construction proceeded apace. Railroad companies operated 1,498 miles of track by 1837. By the end of the 1840s, that figure had increased to 8,021 miles, and it continued to grow vigorously throughout the century.[8]

THE CENTRAL PACIFIC AND THE BIG FOUR

One of the main reasons for funding the transcontinental road, however, was national defense—a rationale that also brought about construction of the federal interstate highway system nearly a century later. The idea of a coast-to-coast link had been discussed in California for some time, but Congress did not approve funds for it until the Civil War was underway. The railroad would be a means not only of hastening shipments to and from California and protecting it from possible attack, but of keeping it loyal to the Union. It did not hurt that the road's main California backers were Free Soil Republicans.

It long had been understood that the federal government would have to assist in bearing the enormous cost of building a transcontinental road. In 1852, the California legislature had asked the state's congressional delegation to seek federal funds for construction, and the requests were repeated in state railroad conventions in 1853 and 1859.[9]

With other Sacramento merchants, Huntington became an advocate of the transcontinental railroad, and gave seed money to an engineer and railroad proponent named Theodore Judah to help convince Congress of its viability. Although the project had been pushed locally for decades, with consistent boosting by California newspapers, most notably the *Sacramento Union*, California was still in its infancy and results had been negligible. At one railroad meeting in 1860, Huntington and Judah had tried to drum up support from Sacramento businessmen, but had received most of their contributions in the form of barrels of flour and sacks of potatoes.

Huntington and his associates nevertheless succeeded in lobbying Congress to enact the first Pacific Railroad Act on 1 July 1862. On 8 January 1863, after forty-six years of discussion, ground was broken for the transcontinental line. The next year, the original railroad act was amended to increase government aid. From 1862 to 1920, the federal government was to give the associates millions of dollars in subsidies and bonds and 10.1 million acres of western lands. The original act of 1862, it should be noted, stipulated that "said Company shall repay said bonds at maturity," the contentions of the associates thirty years later not to the contrary.[10]

In San Francisco, where boosters had indulged in some intramural rivalry with Sacramento's over the project, there was considerable skepticism about Huntington and his colleagues. The suspicion was that the merchant, who had no railroad experience, was interested not so much in running a railroad as in picking the plums of the government's largesse. This apprehension was to be repeated, albeit sixty years later. Daggett has pointed out that money lent in Sacramento then was yielding a whopping and easy return of two percent a month. He has concluded it "very probable," considering the availability of so easy an investment, that Huntington and his partners took on the highly difficult and speculative railroad project because they anticipated an even better profit from the government's bounty.[11]

It was Huntington, nevertheless, who assumed final responsibility for the difficult job of building and running the railroad: Stanford served mainly as a charming but not particularly bright figurehead and political connection, while Crocker functioned as labor overseer. Hopkins looked after, occasionally overlooked, and sometimes cooked the books.

In later years, after the railroad was well established, Huntington returned to the East. He disliked California. One of his pet theories, no doubt informed by his Yankee upbringing, was that the state's mild climate had bred a race of indolent weaklings. In New York, he tended his financial affairs from a Wall Street office, often spending fourteen hours a day there and wearing an odd kind of skullcap that made him look more like a cleric than a financier. Twice a year, he made baronial visits to inspect his California holdings. Of the railroad man's final journey to San Francisco, Arthur McEwen, a Hearst writer who often attacked Huntington, sometimes in his own, short-lived newsletters, described him as "a hard and cheery old man, with no more soul than a shark" and as "a cheerful, frank old pirate who reproves his subjects like a patriarch."[12]

Even his most faithful disciples have had to emphasize that Huntington was a man of action who got things done while conceding that in so doing, "his scruples were highly adaptable."[13] One biographer has gone so far as to attempt to clear Huntington of charges of bribery of public officials and newspaper owners, theorizing that since the bribes were made for the benefit of the company and not for Huntington—itself a somewhat dubious supposition—they were not in fact bribes.[14]

He was a sharp businessman, and his social interests, such as they were, seldom overcame his business sense. "Enterprise for the public good interested him little," Stuart Daggett has written, with some understatement.[15] Summing up the careers of the Big Four, Daggett admits to "a feeling of indignation at the selfishness of these men." Bribery was just one of the tools in their business satchel. They relied just as much on offers of employment, political and personal favors, rate rebates and adjustments, patronage, and frequent reminders to the public of the overall economic benefit of the railroad. Though allowing that the Big Four unquestionably got things done, Daggett concludes that the associates, as they were also sometimes called, "lowered the standard of business ethics of their time"—a standard not particularly high by any measure.[16]

By the middle of the 1890s, Huntington had attained not only regional prominence in the West as the sole surviving member of the Big Four, but a certain national celebrity, to be linked in the public consciousness with other railroad barons like the Goulds and the Vanderbilts. He built a mansion on Fifth Avenue in New York and became a neighbor of the Vanderbilts and the Whitneys. He attempted to reinforce his assault on high society by displaying a family coat of arms in the place, but a *New York World* reporter dispatched by Joseph Pulitzer discovered that the Huntington escutcheon included a buffalo in its design.[17] Like the Huntington coat of arms, Huntington's fame was a strange mixture. The public admired his great wealth and upward rise even as it occasionally questioned his methods.

Near the end of his life, speaking to posterity with one of the historian Hubert Howe Bancroft's scribes as intermediary, Huntington seemed unperturbed. "I am not a sociable man," he explained. "But I get as much out of life as any man in America." He had been attacked by many newspapers, magazines, civic groups, and politicians during his life, but "ridicule and abuse slid off his back as lightly as chaff," one biographer noted.[18]

Huntington was well aware of the value of public opinion, up to a point. He seemed to put a price on it as he might, say, on a sack of potatoes for sale in his dry goods store, or a load of steel for extending his rail lines. He had personally taken an early part in California's newspaper business, participating in the founding of the *Sacramento Times*, the first Free Soil paper in the state. The paper's first editor, James McClatchy, had been ensconced in offices upstairs from the Huntington & Hopkins dry goods store at 54 K Street, Sacramento.[19]

Some years later, Huntington hired the journalist William H. Mills to oversee his press relations in California, and in private communications, at least, he could react rather strongly to adverse opinions in the press. "If I owned the paper, I would control it or burn it," he suggested in a letter to his colleague David A. Colton when queried about one upstart journal in 1876. The advice was contained in one of the famous Colton letters, which gave the public the first real proof of the railroad's corrupt political tactics. The letters had become public as the result of a lawsuit against the railroad by Colton's widow, and appeared in 1883 in the *San Francisco Chronicle*.[20]

After Huntington died in August 1900, his remains were entombed in a large mausoleum near Throg's Neck, New York. The memorial edifice, patterned after a Roman temple, had been five years and $250,000 in the making. At the time of his death, Huntington was director and president of ten companies. Most, like the Southern Pacific, were railroads. He was a director only of seventeen more corporations, including the Western Union Telegraph Company, and had interests, some of them nearly controlling ones, in thirteen other enterprises ranging from the Brooklyn Rapid Transit Company and the Newport News Shipbuilding and Dry Dock Company to the Astoria and Columbia River Railroad Company.[21] His estate was valued at more than $30 million.

OPPOSITION TO THE RAILROAD

In 1877, when Bierce became associate editor of the *Argonaut*, the Central Pacific Railroad had been operating for only eight years but already had become a dominant force in California's politics and economy. The contentions of some of Bierce's biographers notwithstanding, lively if scattered opposition to the railroad's unequal rates and corrupt practices already existed.

The railroad associates, knowing they would be reimbursed by the government, not only had spent lavishly on construction, but kept two sets of books. One historian estimates that the six-year construction phase of the project alone netted them a 500 to 600 percent return on their initial one-million-dollar investment, before a single passenger or pound of freight was hauled.[22]

To pile up government subsidies, spending had been lavish, construction slow, and accounting creative. The associates, not to be outdone by Muhammad, had moved the mountains to themselves, at least on paper. Since the government paid three times the normal rate to compensate for the rigors of alpine construction, the railroad men had surveyors fix the California side of the Sierra Nevada range many miles west of its customary boundary, and reaped substantial rewards for the comparatively easy work in the lower country.

Though some citizens had become angry as word of the railroad's swindles inevitably leaked out, nothing much came of that anger besides a certain amount of sound and fury. Outraged articles and editorials were published and investigations were launched of the Contract and Finance Company, as the company's construction arm was called. It turned out the company had kept two sets of books, one listing imaginative prices for services rendered. The truer accounting never surfaced, figuratively or literally, for it apparently had ended up in a river, possibly the Seine. The government did not get any money back, although two construction engineers later testifed that the road could have been built for about one-quarter of its actual cost.[23]

In part, the railroad may have owed some of its immunity from public attack to the warm but fading regard engendered by its passenger service. Even in the early 1870s, the luxury of being able to cross the continent in ten days in relative peace and comfort, give or take a few bumps and accidents, remained something of a marvel.

Still, plenty of cause for concern remained even beyond the phony books. As early as 1868, it became clear that the Central Pacific was intent on holding the early monopoly it was to enjoy in much of the state.[24] By threatening, cajoling, or buying out prospective competitors and buying all terminals at the major shipping hub of the San Francisco Bay, the associates gave themselves the opportunity to earn substantial operating income beyond the government subsidies they were already enjoying.

Monopoly gave Huntington and his colleagues the ability to exercise Huntington's stated business theory of charging all the market would bear. For many years the invisible hand that regulates the marketplace under classical capitalist theory remained not only invisible but nonexistent, and a strictly theoretical proposition for the associates. Of the six other transcontinental railroads that were formed after the Central Pacific, none managed to reach San Francisco until the Santa Fe got an independent connection—three decades after the Central Pacific had started running its trains.[25]

A general outcry arose over the railroad's high and unfair rates. The disenchantment was fanned by the severe economic depression that gripped the state in 1877, just as Bierce was taking up his position as a columnist and associate editor for the weekly *Argonaut*. Even before that, rumblings of discontent had been evident. In 1868, the year before Stanford swung and missed his first strike at the final spike, Henry George had warned against the advent of railroads in the *Overland Monthly* (which Bierce often called the *Warmedoverland Monthly*). George did not fear political corruption, but argued that the increasing wealth and population trains would bring to the West would despoil Eden, leading to the same economic and social problems that bedeviled the East Coast and Europe. The value of land would inevitably rise, pushing it beyond the means of the common man.[26]

The railroad became a power in the state even before one paying train had traversed its tracks, and some newspapers accumulated political and economic capital by making a great show of opposing it. In the same year that George gave voice to his forebodings, the de Young family converted the *San Francisco Chronicle* from a theater sheet to a general daily, promising in the lead editorial on 1 September that "neither the Republican party nor the Democratic party, nor the Pacific Railroad, nor the Bank of California, are great enough to frighten us or rich enough to buy us."[27]

Still, the mood of the press was usually friendly. Even as the road's *raison d'être*, the Civil War, began to fade in memory, the city began to prepare itself for the influx of immigrants expected to arrive with the trains. Editorial calls went forth for civic improvements to accommodate the anticipated Eastern hordes. Newspapers stood to benefit financially from these new consumers and possible subscribers, of course, and through the 1860s, they remained receptive to the railroad, despite some dissent over the copious funds doled out to Huntington and his cronies.[28]

Opposition to the railroad increased in the 1870s, however, as citizens began to see the associates' dirty methods and attempts at preserving their young monopoly in action. Several editorials, possibly written by Henry George, appeared in the *Chronicle* from 1870 to 1873 and decried the railroad's huge land holdings received gratis from the federal government.[29] At about the same time, passengers and others began to complain about the dangers of the trains' poor brakes and faulty equipment, which already had caused a number of fatalities.[30]

In 1871, a convention of citizens in San Francisco—a city still envious of the railroad's Sacramento roots—"openly denounced railroad abuses and demanded that they should be abated."[31] That same year, Californians elected a governor and legislature that were violently anti-railroad. The legislators' opposition to the railroad, however, tended to be more spirited in front of the electorate than behind closed doors with the railroad's owners.

One newspaper editor, Bierce's one-time colleague on the *Argonaut* and later nemesis, Jerome Hart, pointed out that the supposedly anti-railroad legislature had elected a pro-railroad man to the United States Senate. He was returned to the Senate by yet another anti-railroad legislature some years later. "For popular consumption," Hart was forced to conclude, an anti-railroad stance "was all right." Sardonically, he remembered those early stands against the railroad: "All California legislatures then were anti-railroad. Can it be that a California legislature in the seventies was insincere in its opposition to 'the railroad'? But no—no one can believe that."[32]

Despite the railroad's strong position, the associates remained vigilant and could take decisive action when confronted with real dissension. The *Sacramento Union* had supported an anti-railroad candidate named Newton Booth for governor in 1871. Angered, Huntington acquired control of the rival *Sacramento Record* and put his new press agent, Mills, in charge of it. The *Record* was to make war on the *Union* and also to help bolster the price of railroad stock and counter increasing public hostility. Central Pacific agents advised local merchants and railroad car shop owners to withdraw their advertisements from the *Union*. By December 1874, the Union, deprived of its railroad subsidies and many of its ads, was forced into foreclosure. The paper was sold to a lawyer and merged in 1875 with Huntington's Record. The Record-Union was to remain a railroad organ through the time of Huntington's death twenty-five years later.[33]

John Miller, a former clerk, ticket agent, and assistant accountant for the Contract and Finance Company, whipped up public rancor and confirmed certain suspicions in 1871 when he publicly revealed that the railroad had improperly collected millions of dollars from the federal government. In the same year, a paper in the interior, the *Stockton Independent*, was attacking the railroad, and by the middle of the decade, farmers in the Central Valley were complaining of the railroad's high and seemingly arbitrary rates.

In 1874 and again in 1876, the legislature tried but failed to brake the railroad's rates.[34] It did manage, in 1876, to pass the O'Connor Act, which set up a railroad commission. Like many later acts and commissions, they were limited in effect. The law was gutted by the next legislature, and the commission replaced by a sole commissioner who was merely authorized to gather information but not to act or even to make recommendations for action.[35]

Newspaper publishers meanwhile had discovered that while the railroad offered patronage and advertising enticements, those benefits had to be weighed against the circulation gains they could make by playing to the increasingly anti-railroad feelings of the public. This became especially clear during the severe depression in 1877, which followed wild speculation in mining stocks and the inevitable collapse not only of stocks but of some major banks as well.

In that year, for instance, the publisher of the *San Francisco Bulletin* brought a libel suit against the publishers of the *San Francisco Chronicle*. The de Youngs had damaged his paper's standing, the publisher claimed, by accusing the *Bulletin* of being "secretly friendly to the Southern Pacific Railroad," despite an outward face of antagonism. The publicity value of simply making such charges was the real point. Such legal battles were common and reflected attempts by editors to discredit rivals and build circulation.[36]

During the depression, Denis Kearney formed the Workingmen's Party in San Francisco. These "sandlotters," so called for the angry public meetings they held in vacant sandlots around the city, talked of sacking the palatial mansions the Big Four had built atop Nob Hill. Although Kearney had boldly promised a workingman's revolt, he and his men never stormed any lofty barricades. They had to settle for harassing the city's more accessible and ubiquitous (and less fearsome) Chinese immigrants, competitors in the labor market whom the luckless Irish also blamed for their troubles.

Bierce returned from his pleasant literary interlude in England at the height of the sandlot hooliganism. The contrast between London and San Francisco must have been great, and some writers have suggested that Kearney's bullying and mob tactics ultimately made Bierce suspicious of all social causes.[37] By this time, opposition to the railroad was not limited to such extremists, but had become general. One historian claims that by 1878, scarcely a decade after the railroad had been so eagerly anticipated, nine out of ten citizens held it in low regard.[38]

Despite his rough methods, Kearney was popular with some newspapers, which likened him to a Cassius leading the masses against the

Roman elite. In 1878, the *Sacramento Bee* and a more radical sheet, the *Sacramento Sun*, backed a state constitutional convention that would put restraints on the railroad.[39] At the convention, which lasted from September 1878 to March 1879, the railroad was the main concern, although the delegates also wrestled with problems like corporate power, taxation, corrupt politics, and Chinese immigration. The convention eventually created a railroad commission and a state board of equalization, which again failed in their supposed mission to force upon the railroad equitable property taxes and freight rates. Once again, the state's legislators were ready to limit the commissioners' efforts if they showed any sign of harming the railroad's interests.[40]

Railroads had owed their initial construction in great part to a press campaign, and their owners continued to manipulate the press to their own ends long after construction had ceased. Using their economic and political power, they crushed such small buds of newspaper opposition that emerged. Still, opposition was never entirely snuffed out. Though Bierce has often been portrayed as a lonely crusader against the Central Pacific, his attacks were not without precedent. But these attackers tended to vacillate or weaken before the power of the corporation.

Huntington and, to a lesser extent, the rest of the Big Four presented ideal subjects for satire, not only in their physical appearance but in the smug hypocrisy they shared. Bierce's sharp pen made an ideal instrument for poking through the veil of lies the railroad had drawn over itself and its friends, but he needed a publisher who would support such a risky enterprise.

NOTES

1. Oscar Lewis, *The Big Four* (New York: Alfred A. Knopf, 1969), 241.

2. Ibid., 214.

3. Cerinda W. Evans, *Collis Potter Huntington* (Newport News: The Mariners' Museum), 2:675.

4. Thomas Beer, *The Mauve Decade* (New York: Alfred A. Knopf, 1926), 83.

5. Lewis, 213.

6. James A. Ward, *Railroads and the Character of America, 1820–1887* (Knoxville: University of Tennessee Press, 1986), 7–9, 15–17, 105.

7. Ronald Takaki, *Iron Cages: Race and Culture in Nineteenth-Century America* (New York: Alfred A. Knopf, 1979), 169.

8. Ward, 13–14, 80.

9. Stuart Daggett, *Chapters on the History of the Southern Pacific* (New York: The Ronald Press Co., 1922), 45.

10. Ibid., 54, 58.

11. Ibid., 15–16, 51.

12. Lewis, 211.

13. David Lavender, *The Great Persuader* (Garden City, N.Y.: Doubleday & Co., 1970), 376.

14. Ibid., 366.

15. Daggett, 11.

16. Ibid., 220–221, 455–458.

17. W. A. Swanberg, *Whitney Father, Whitney Heiress* (New York: Charles Scribner's Sons, 1980), 70, 77.

18. Lewis, 231, 212.

19. Evans, 1:38.

20. Daggett, 201.

21. Evans, 2:657–658.

22. Daggett, 81.

23. Ibid., 68.

24. Ibid., 104.

25. Ibid., 275–77.

26. Sarah Lee Sharp, "Social Criticism in California During the Gilded Age" (Ph.D. dissertation, University of California, San Diego, 1979), 231–233.

27. John Bruce, *Gaudy Century: The Story of San Francisco's Hundred Years of Robust Journalism* (New York: Random House, 1948), 141.

28. John P. Young, *Journalism in California* (San Francisco: Chronicle Publishing Co., 1915), 74.

29. Ibid., 79.

30. Frank A. Leach, *Recollections of a Newspaperman* (San Francisco: Samuel Levinson, 1917), 155.

31. Young, 124–125.

32. Jerome Hart, *In Our Second Century* (San Francisco: The Pioneer Press, 1931), 127.

33. Evans, 1:189–190; Fremont Older, *Growing Up* (San Francisco: San Francisco Call-Bulletin, 1931), 69.

34. Daggett, 182.

35. Sharp, 30.

36. Hart, 117.

37. Carey McWilliams, *Ambrose Bierce: A Biography* (New York: Albert & Charles Boni, 1929), 135.

38. Lewis, 140.

39. Sharp, 85–89.

40. Ibid., 26–27; Young, 95, 124–125.

Ambrose Bierce. Courtesy of Department of Special Collections, Stanford University Libraries.

Officers of the Central Pacific Railroad. Courtesy of California State Railroad Museum.

COLLAPSE OF COLLIS.

This is how Davenport views the knock-out of Huntington by Bierce. At the anti-funding jubilee last night the name of Mr. Bierce was frequently applauded, because of his vigorous efforts against the infamous refunding measure of the Pacific Railroads.

A Homer Davenport cartoon from the *Examiner* depicts Bierce besting Huntington during the funding bill fight of 1896. Courtesy of San Francisco Academy of Comic Art Collection, The Ohio State University Cartoon Research Library.

"Ah, that we could fall into women's arms without falling into their hands." Courtesy of Department of Special Collections, Stanford University Library.

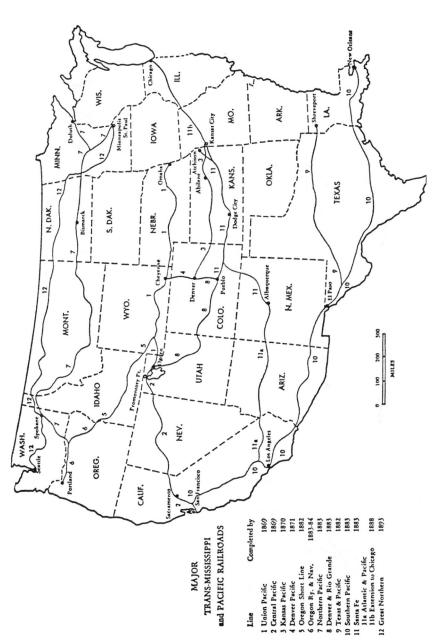

MAJOR TRANS-MISSISSIPPI and PACIFIC RAILROADS

Line	Completed by
1 Union Pacific	1869
2 Central Pacific	1869
3 Kansas Pacific	1870
4 Denver Pacific	1871
5 Oregon Short Line	1882
6 Oregon Ry. & Nav.	1883-84
7 Northern Pacific	1883
8 Denver & Rio Grande	1883
9 Texas & Pacific	1882
10 Southern Pacific	1883
11 Santa Fe	1883
11a Atlantic & Pacific	1888
11b Extension to Chicago	1893
12 Great Northern	1893

Central and Southern Pacific and completion dates in nineteenth century. From *American Railroads* by J. Stover. Copyright © 1961, 1997 by The University of Chicago. Used by permission of the publisher, The University of Chicago Press.

6

Argonaut and *Wasp*

Between 1877 and 1886, Bierce worked at two San Francisco periodicals, the *Argonaut* and the *Wasp*. He displayed markedly different attitudes to the railroad in each, reflecting the antipodal political natures of the periodicals and of the changing times more than a change in his own thinking. As a writer and associate editor for the *Argonaut*, which was a staunch supporter of the railroad, Bierce tended to ignore the Octopus in his weekly column, and occasionally, in an offhand way, to hurl small brickbats at the railroad's opponents. Several years later, as editor of the satirical *Wasp*, he adopted a much more caustic tone. His real, published antagonism to the railroad began then.

A difference in editorial outlook explains much. E. C. Macfarlane, managing editor and eventually publisher of the *Wasp*, long a Democratic-leaning journal, had no ties to the railroad, unlike the editor of the Republican-friendly *Argonaut*, Frank Pixley, who was a crony of Stanford. As editor of the *Wasp*, Bierce also enjoyed more autonomy than he had as associate editor of the *Argonaut*. Macfarlane often consulted with Bierce and deferred to his judgment. Bierce produced much of the *Wasp's* contents, generating enormous amounts of material in all-night writing sessions.

Some of Bierce's antagonism toward the railroad may have been caused by anger at his old editor, Pixley, who had refused to take him back on the *Argonaut* when he returned from his failed mining venture in the Dakota Territory. Also, journalism and the times had changed, and the public had become even more receptive to criticism of the railroad. When Bierce worked on the *Argonaut* in the 1870s, San Francisco journalism was often execrable, still groggy from the hangover of its booster days, and the railroad, perhaps the foremost beneficiary of boosterism, still enjoyed a certain immunity from criticism. One favorite theme of the *Wasp* under Bierce was that sort of feeble writing and reporting, and he filled the *Wasp's* pages with parodies of society notes and other journalistic fluff.

Growing public anger at the railroad helped support Bierce's attacks. The corruption of railroad and public officials was becoming better known and the economic hard times of the 1870s and a massacre of protesting farmers at Mussel Slough in 1880 had made the railroad many more enemies.

In the *Wasp*, Bierce often slashed at the railroad in editorials and scattered bits of unsigned parody that he almost certainly wrote. His antagonism also was evident, though less prevalent, in his weekly column of "Prattle," which he had carried over from the *Argonaut*. The form of each type of writing explains the difference. Editorials were allotted much more space and often occupied an entire page or two in the *Wasp*. "Prattle" relied on brevity and wit. It usually consisted of only a column or two of unrelated paragraphs, each commenting sardonically on a public event of the day. The greater space assigned the editorials let them address the more complex processes of the railroad's political and economic programs, while the brevity of "Prattle" was more suitable for quick stabs at the personalities of the Big Four.

"PRATTLER" AND "PRATTLE" IN THE *ARGONAUT*

When Bierce assumed his duties at the *Argonaut* in 1877, the public already held the railroad in some disregard. Not only did farmers and radical workingmen oppose it for economic reasons, but the general public was becoming increasingly concerned about its dishonesty, corruption, and pilferage of the public treasury. Yet in three years of providing the *Argonaut* with his weekly column, first titled "The Prattler" and then shortened to "Prattle," Bierce mentioned the railroad only four times and then only in joshing terms. He wrote in a short, breezy style, devoting most of his space to small jokes, ironic comments on items gleaned from other newspapers, and attacks against journalists, poets, preachers, and other minor local luminaries.

Rather than firing any shots at the railroad's methods or management, Bierce took a practically neutral stance on the issue, using bits of railroad material to fashion japes for his readers' amusement. Occasionally, he attacked those who opposed the railroad, but these jabs had more to do with sneering at the country roots of farmers and Grangers upset about freight costs than with actually defending the railroad.

His first mention of the railroad facetiously noted that it "was not so bad after all." Its plan to plant a quarter of a million eucalyptus trees in California to produce a crop of railroad ties was acceptable even though the eucalyptus was a "pestilent vegetable." The railroad, Bierce explained, did not wish thereby to poison the atmosphere for everyone in the state, but only wanted "to kill off the grangers . . . many of whom are opposed to railways." Bierce implied that the farmers were a backward and troublesome lot, fully as "pestilent" as the eucalyptus.[1]

Noting a suggestion by the state railroad commissioners that conductors be empowered to act as deputy sheriffs in the counties through which their trains were passing, he quipped in another column: "Nonsense! A conductor has already the power to arrest a whole train."[2] He also made jokes at the expense of some of the desolate valley towns and counties the road served: "A probably fatal accident occurred the other day on the Central Pacific Railroad. A passenger who had got off the train at Lathrop by mistake decided to settle there."[3]

Newspaper journalism in California in the 1870s has been described, with some justification, as "beneath contempt."[4] Standards were low, money often short. Boosterism, though subdued compared to previous decades, was still common. Bierce's reticence about attacking the railroad may have been partly a result of the low journalistic integrity of the time. It also derived in part from his disgust at the actions of Kearney's mobs. Even though he attacked the sandlotters, he showed comparatively little compassion for their Chinese victims or for any kind of reform movement. His columns in the *Argonaut* do not wholly bear out the contentions of those who claim that Bierce held what might be called enlightened and liberal racial views. In one, he facetiously recommended ending labor unrest by "putting a Chinaman in the hole and watching to see if he came up in Peru."[5]

Even at this relatively early stage in his career, Bierce was not looking to reformers for solutions. He traced most social problems to innate shortcomings of character common to most if not all individuals, rather than to any broad theory of social injustice. Noting a lecture by railroad opponent Henry George titled "Why Work Is Scarce, Wages Are Low, and Labor Is Restless," Bierce offered his own answer: "Because indolence is agreeable, talk cheap, and whisky disquieting."[6]

The anti-Irish, anti-Catholic *Argonaut*, in fact, had been founded to drive the labor leader Kearney out of California, just as the Irishman wished to drive the Chinese out.[7] The railroad's owners and Kearney's men were enemies, and the *Argonaut* routinely defended the railroad in editorials.

Frank Pixley, the *Argonaut's* editor and publisher, was a wealthy Republican and old friend of Stanford who had served as state treasurer when Stanford was governor. By one account, Pixley had participated with one of Stanford's brothers in an effective and not unusual method of campaigning at the time, filling his pockets with gold coins on the mornings of primary elections and heading out to mold public opinion in a most direct and convincing way.[8] Pixley hoped some day to be governor himself and knew that friendly relations with a wealthy kingmaker like the railroad might further his cause. Given his boss's position and political aspirations, it would have been nearly impossible for Bierce to make a serious attack on the railroad and keep his job.

Although Bierce toed the line by refraining from attacking the railroad, it should be noted that he wrote nothing in support of the corporation during his tenure at the *Argonaut*. None of its obsequious editorial matter spilled over into "Prattle." The closest thing was Bierce's jest at the expense of the farmers. But this small joke also hinted at the railroad's rough methods. And it just as likely reflected Bierce's pride in his acquired city manners and his revulsion for anything that smacked of the farm.

THE *WASP*

Back in San Francisco after his fruitless expedition into the gold fields of the Dakota Territory, Bierce applied for his old job at Frank Pixley's *Argonaut* and was turned down. The exact reason for the rejection has not been recorded. Possibly the rebuff grew out of Bierce's difficult temperament or iconoclastic political and social views, though it might just as easily have been caused by a lack of openings or by a certain editorial doubtfulness about Bierce's appeal to readers. According to the not always reliable Hart, Pixley "said that Bierce's disappearance from its pages had made no impression on the *Argonaut's* readers."[9]

Soon, in January 1881, Bierce found work with a young satirical weekly called the Wasp. Pixley's rejection, however, had cut him badly at a time when he was trying to recover from his disappointing trip to the Black Hills. During his tenure at the *Wasp*, which lasted into 1886,

Bierce often attacked his former boss and Pixley's old friend and bene-factor, Leland Stanford.

A signal event in the railroad's history had taken place during Bierce's absence from California. A group of farmers in the state's Central Valley, then devoted largely to wheat growing, had banded together to protest the railroad's high-handed tactics in raising the price of land it had promised to sell them. After the railroad got an eviction order, the farmers were still in a fighting mood. The railroad sent a United States marshal as well as its own agents, including two hired gunfighters, to force the matter to a conclusion. Seven men died at what came to be known as the Mussel Slough Massacre.[10] The picture of railroad thugs killing farmers was not an appealing one. Public opposition to the rail-road, slowly on the rise for nearly a decade, crested to new heights as Bierce settled into his new editorship.

The *Wasp* had been founded by three Czech immigrants who are better known today for a brand of champagne produced under the family name. Francis, Anton, and Joseph Korbel had arrived in California in the 1860s and made a living manufacturing cigar boxes and labels and operating a winery near the Russian River. Despite the fulsome re-ports of the booster press, California was not then an Eden even for foreign immigrants seeking to escape the troubles of their own coun-tries. Upset by widespread political corruption as well as by the violent confrontations between capital and labor in their adopted homeland, the brothers founded the *Wasp* in 1876.

From the start, the journal was an unusual one. Practically all pe-riodicals at the time were printed in black and white, but the *Wasp* was lavish in its use of color. It owed its unique appearance to the family's cigar box business. The same artists who designed the Korbels' labels were put to work designing colorful political caricatures for the sheet. The *Wasp* may have been the first magazine in the United States to use color illustrations regularly.[11]

The magazine's ownership changed the month that Bierce took over, however, when it was acquired by a front man representing Charles Webb Howard. Bierce apparently was unaware that the president of a local and corrupt utility called the Spring Valley Water Company had become the real owner of the *Wasp*. Early in 1883, when Bierce decided to attack the utility for its flagrant bribes of local politicians, his pub-lisher, Macfarlane, a member of a Hawaiian sugar-growing family, had to intervene and explain the delicacy of the situation. Bierce apparently refused to back down. Soon after, in March 1883, Macfarlane bought the *Wasp*, after rejecting a condition that he refrain from attacking the water company in the future. During the next few years, the periodical came closest to deserving its name. Public sinners–they had many callings, but most were politicians—were pilloried mercilessly. The combination of Bierce's acid pen and the wicked caricatures of the *Wasp's* artists was splendid and devastating.

Despite the *Wasp's* great flair, Macfarlane sold it in 1885 to a newspaperman named Colonel J. P. Jackson. Jackson, owner of the *San Francisco Evening Post*, milked the magazine of much of its venom. It became a humor sheet similar to others like *Judge* and *Life*. Rather than impaling public victims with wit, the periodical began trying to entertain readers with gentle joshing and folksy humor. It also began to accept ads for patent medicines, which, along with all other "questionable ads," previous owners had sternly refused.

Bierce did not last long under Jackson's rule. Before the takeover, the style of writing in the *Wasp* suggests that Bierce sometimes nearly filled it with his own stuff. After the change in ownership, his contribution subsided to his weekly column of "Prattle." Within a few months, he was gone entirely. His last column appeared on 11 September 1886, in the same edition in which the *Wasp* was touting a supposed circulation of 16,000 and claiming for itself the peculiar distinction of being "the largest of any pictorial paper published west of the Rocky Mountains."[12]

Though nearly all the contents of the magazine were unsigned, it is almost certain that Bierce wrote much of its editorial content from 1881 to 1885, and that his contributions fell off to practically nothing after Jackson's purchase. Bierce's writing style is unique and unmistakable, keen, literate, and rich in allusion. It was aggressive even by the ornery standards of journalism in San Francisco in the 1880s, when editors pinned some of their circulation hopes on the spectacle they could create by trading verbal swipes with other editors.[13]

"PRATTLE" IN THE *WASP*

Despite the freedom and political support his new position offered him, Bierce's attacks on the railroad in "Prattle" during the Wasp years were nevertheles remarkably limited. Over a span of more than five years, the column contained only ten items dealing with the railroad or its principals. In keeping with "Prattle's" format at the time— ironic squibs, each seldom running more than a paragraph or two—mentions of the railroad tended to be brief and light.

Two items attacked Charles Crocker, who had managed the road's construction and who was mainly responsible for labor relations. Three composed as ditties and verses undertook the more general goal of ridiculing the wicked ways of the railroad and, more specifically, of its owners. Four examined the railroad and the press, to the detriment of both. Another addressed railroad safety.

The references to Crocker resembled physical assaults. One poked at his great girth, with a subtle jab at the simple-minded booster articles of the country press, many of which were sponsored by the railroad and, in some cases, written by railroad officials. Noting that the *Gridley Herald* of Butte County "has been made happy by the discovery of a mushroom more than nine feet in circumference," Bierce calculated that, though Crocker weighed 225 pounds, he would still outweigh the "mammoth fungus of our exultant contemporary" even if "the weight of the fat belonging to the public" were deducted.[14]

In another slice at Crocker, Bierce refuted a familiar defense of the railroad: that the ends of universal and modern transportation justified the means of monopoly, coercion, and corruption. Such logic was nonsense, Bierce retorted. Crocker's "great and permanent value to the State" was only selfishness, "merely a natural instinct inherited from his public spirited ancestor, the man who dug the postholes on Mount Calvary."[15]

Bierce's poetic taunts of the railroad ran from light parodies to macabre dirges. A medley of revised nursery rhymes included this jab:

Hey diddle, diddle, the cat's got the fiddle,
The cow jumped over the moon.
The railroad man laughs at such trivial sport
And will pocket the four of them soon.[16]

Noting that the tool that had been used to start construction of the Central Pacific was on exhibit at the New Orleans Exposition, Bierce composed an ironic ode to the "historic spade":

Within thee, as within a magic glass,
I seem to see a foul procession pass—
Judges with ermine dragging in the mud
And spotted here and there with guiltless blood;
Gold-greedy legislators jingling bribes,
Kept editors and sycophantic scribes;
Liars in swarms and plunderers in tribes.[17]

Bierce aimed most of his other attacks at the railroad, the press, and their symbiotic relationship. In one, he implicitly criticized the press's eagerness to accept a railroad superintendent's weak explanation that an accident had occurred on a well-traveled section between San Francisco and Port Costa because "the track is always warm." Bierce responded by listing "a ghastly record of preventible accidents caused due to carelessness on the part of the railroad people" and concluded that "with a warm track and a Division Superintendent who is perilous at any temperature, we must expect a good deal of killing on this end of the line."[18]

The society columns of San Francisco newspapers were laden with accounts of the social maneuvers of leading citizens in minute detail, and Bierce regularly parodied the breathless, inane reports. He ridiculed the *Argonaut* when it pandered to the nouveau riche railroad aristocracy by introducing a column of "Railroad Personals"—bits of society chaff aimed at stroking railroad magnates' egos. Here was a chance to swat three enemies and three hypocritical pretensions in one blow—high society, the railroad, and Pixley—and Bierce did not hesitate: "If there be a spittle that no dog will lick, lead Thou this Pixley to that unthinkable discharge, and rub his reluctant nose in it."[19]

In other columns, he pointed to an even more direct connection between the railroad and the press, and a not uncommon one. In one, for instance, he mentioned that the railroad's nominee for governor intended to buy the *San Francisco Alta* and make it into a "railroad organ."[20]

Bierce's attacks on the railroad in "Prattle" were sparse and in themselves light and brief, even by the standards of a column that depended on brevity for effect. Much of his writing in "Prattle" during this period concentrated on the failings of other journalists, as did much of his writing elsewhere in the *Wasp*. He had plenty of material at hand. Despite nostalgic feelings that some moderns harbor for supposedly better newspapers in past times, the quality of the nineteenth-century press in California was frequently awful and fully merited Bierce's attacks. Part of this tendency may also be attributed to a fact of nineteenth-century San Francisco newspaper life mentioned earlier: competition was intense and journalists frequently slighted competitors. Bierce's rancor may also have represented his resentment at having to return to journalism after his failed attempt at economic escape in the Dakota Territory. His personal and professional bitterness is certainly evident in his attacks on Pixley and the *Argonaut*.

THE EDITORIALS

Mentions of the railroad appeared much more frequently in the *Wasp's* unsigned editorials than in "Prattle." At least thirty ran during Bierce's tenure as editor and he almost certainly wrote all but one. Not only were these attacks more numerous. They also tended to be much longer than the snippets in "Prattle." Some took all of the editorials' weekly allotment of space, usually one page and never more than two.

The editorials differed from "Prattle" in content as well as in form. Though they also employed satire and wit, they tended to provide broader arguments against the railroad and to appeal to the groups most at its mercy. For the first time, Bierce noted the huge loans the railroad had taken from the United States government and demanded their repayment. He singled out San Francisco merchants as victims of the railroad's monopoly tactics, political payoffs, and high and often discriminatory rates. These two factors—the increasing political power of an irate group of city merchants, and the railroad's huge debts to the government—eventually led to its defeat in the funding bill debate in the next decade.

Even though many of the editorials exposed the political, economic, and social damage done by the railroad, they did not neglect the individuals who operated the financial and political levers of the great corporation. They also sympathized with victims, who included not only the usual aggregates of outraged merchants, disconsolate farmers, and displaced laborers, but lesser-known individuals like orphans and restaurant owners who had had the misfortune to stand in the corporation's way and to be crushed. Meanwhile, like "Prattle," the editorials continued to chip away at the railroad's domination not only of both major political parties but of most of the state's newspapers as well.

Villains

As in "Prattle," the editorials attacked individual members of the Big Four, with the notable exception of Mark Hopkins—the elderly bookkeeper who, though not without his faults, alone escaped the wrath of both contemporaries and future generations.

A few of these attacks did not appear as editorials, but filled space in the rest of the magazine as mere squibs. Some parodied poetry or drama or contemporary newspapers, as in this section of "Longfellow Revised by Huntington" taking off from the poet's "Psalm of Life":

> Not enjoyment and not sorrow
> Is our destined end or way;
> I must steal in land to-morrow
> Double what I stole to-day.[21]

Other pasquinades attacked not only the double dealing of the railroad owners but the obsequious and convoluted style of its kept San Francisco editors. One such parody began with the announcement that "Mr. Stealand Standfirm sought the ear of a *Call* reporter." After Standfirm found that appendage in a vacant lot "doing duty as a circus tent for a troupe of strolling religious revivalists" and placed it over himself "like a diving bell," the interview began. Standfirm glibly recounted his philosophy of philanthropy by explaining that he hoped to "obtain at a cheap rate the lasting fame of one who returns to A ten per cent of the money that belongs to B" and by "giving away with my left hand the money that I get by robbing with my right."[22] Elsewhere, Bierce published an "open letter" from "Stealand Landford" to "Crank F. Fixley," in which Landford reminded the editor that "you know me to be a thief but are employed to say I am not."[23]

Bierce did not confine his blows to Stanford nor his references to exposing the railroad's theft and editorial payoffs. He greeted the news of Crocker's planned departure to New York with a left-handed farewell, regretting that Crocker could not, "like a snail," take his Nob Hill mansion with him, and went on to delineate his slimy path of destruction in exacting detail:

To the removal of himself and all his belongings from among a people whose generous encouragement he has punished by plunder—from a state whose industries he has impoverished, whose legislation he has sophisticated and perverted, whose courts of justice he has corrupted, of whose servants he has made thieves and in the debauchery of whose politics he has experienced a coarse delight irrelative to the selfish advantage that was its purpose—from a city whose social tone he has done his best to lower to the level of his own brutal graces, and for whose moral standards he has tried to substitute the fatty degeneration of his own heart,—to the taking of his offensive personality out of contact with a community interpenetrated with the unclean emanation that he calls his influence, we trust he will address himself with such energy and activity as two laborious decades of public and private sinning have left him the ability to invoke.[24]

Victims

By the time Bierce came to the *Wasp*, many Californians, especially San Franciscans, were well aware of the railroad's incursions against farmers, laborers, and merchants. In editorials, Bierce paid due tribute to each of these interest groups. Like the muckrakers, he was indulging his readers in a twice-told tale. But he occasionally singled out the troubles of less familiar individuals who had run afoul of the railroad, recounting the meanness of their misfortunes in something approaching Dickensian style.

One editorial item, for instance, recounted "the robbing of an orphan" by "Messrs. Stanford, Crocker, and Huntington." Through an agent acting in court as a guardian, the railroad had taken title to a valuable piece of land in downtown San Francisco that had passed from James H. Hodgdon to his infant son, A. L. Hodgdon, after the father's death. Fortunately for the child, a judge who later became a prominent figure in the campaign against the railroad's funding bill plan declared the transfer null and void.[25]

Another editorial declared that the railroad had "never done anything smaller and meaner" than what it had done to the owner of a restaurant in the Central Valley town of Lathrop—the same town Bierce had spoofed in the *Argonaut* as a kind of end of the world for any passenger debarking there. The railroad had leased a parcel of land near the depot to a pair of restaurateurs who had "for a long time conducted the business there of promoting dyspepsia and disseminating death, hell and the grave." When a competitor named Shannon set up a restaurant on an adjacent lot he had purchased from the railroad, "vending a milder form of indigestion at a more sufferable rate," the company denied him the right to advertise his fare to passengers waiting on the platform. Finally it went so far as to lease the platform to Shannon's competitors. The legality of the move depended on "the sympathies of the judge," Bierce declared, but morally, "the action of the railroad people is little better than total depravity, but not quite as good as congenital sin."[26]

Bierce's hatred of the railroad was so great that he even threw a sop to laborers, a group he had long distrusted. Though he often had attacked not only Kearney but the entire local labor movement as a collection of drunken, shiftless, and selfish thugs, his dramatic parody "Railroad Comedy in One Act" finds Crocker and Stanford, their names unmangled for once, discussing how to cut costs during difficult economic times. Stanford has a suggestion:

So be it then, clerks, bosses, engineers,
Men who have served faithfully and well,
Whose best years in our service were consumed,
Whose whole dependence lies upon the wage,
We give them for their earnest work.
All these must go.[27]

Social Concerns

Readers occasionally took Bierce to task for his personal attacks on the railroad's owners rather than on the corporation itself. For Bierce, however, the corporation was merely a construct, a fuzzy, abstract "marker" under which the owners could hide. He reasoned that "if the corporation is a thief it is because Stanford, Crocker and Huntington have stolen." The problem lay not in the system but in the individuals that comprised it.

In the same column Bierce professed little hope of solving the conundrum of human dishonesty, claiming that the *Wasp* had no "mission" other than that of spreading the truth. Though he denied the *Wasp* was "making a fight" against the railroad or its owners, one of the metaphors he employed to support his point about individual responsibility seemed to suggest otherwise: "There are such things as armies, but the killing and burning and devastation is done by soldiers, and these are the chaps we shoot at in battle."[28]

Bierce himself moved beyond personal attacks. He illustrated in detail the railroad's monopoly tactics, including the "pools" it formed with other railroads to dampen competition.[29] As early as 1882, he pointed out that, despite the loyalty of many newspaper editors bought by railroad subsidies, local merchants had been antagonized by the monopoly "to the point of open revolt."[30] In 1884, noting that the railroad was in a financially weakened state, he complained that a trip on a passenger train was "a little better than a wagon but not as good as a saddle mule." Listing the even heavier transportation woes of San Francisco merchants as well as of Central Valley farmers, fruit growers, and vintners, he called on them to seize upon their opponent's weak state and to "combine to resist the monstrous extractions of this modern Minotaur."[31]

In other editorials, he rejected the often repeated notion that the railroad owners had earned their wealth and position. They had not, he maintained, because the public, via the United States Treasury, had financed the entire operation—Bierce's answer to the laissez-faire argument, common at the time, that the railroad men had the right to charge all the market could bear. If they had really set up the railroad on their own and operated in a truly free market, perhaps. But Congress had enriched the railroad men with public subsidies, public loans, and public land. The federal government had exercised the right of eminent domain in their behalf and had provided United States Army troops to protect their holdings. Bierce concluded that "to say in any form that property so created and so circumstanced ought to be put on the same footing in respect of control as property that is the creature of private capital and unaided effort is to be some kind of fool."[32]

As early as 1884, he was warning that Huntington, Crocker, and Stanford would neither repay the railroad's debt to the government nor submit to foreclosure, despite the predictions of some newspaper contemporaries that they would turn over their property to satisfy the debt.[33] He also harped on efforts by the railroad to cut its property taxes by means of heavy lobbying in the California legislature, noting again that the effort was applauded by the usual claque of newspaper supporters.[34]

Given the corrupt condition of local politics, it should not be surprising that Bierce had little faith in any legislative solution. Rather, what faith he had he put in the banding together of injured interests—mainly the merchants. He often spotlighted the railroad's control of the two-party system and the feeble efforts by the parties to give the public the verisimilitude of regulating their railroad master. An anti-monopoly measure introduced in the 1884 Republican state convention, he pointed out, was "meaningless."[35] As for the Democratic Party: it "ought to be served with a writ of *quo warranto* and made to show whence it derives its authority to represent the anti-railroad element in our state politics." Its elected representatives had "stubbornly withheld from the railroad crowd everything that they didn't want."[36]

Stanford's senatorial aspirations horrified Bierce, not least because the corrupt California legislature hand-picked the state's United States senators. Bierce's comment on the object of Stanford's desire was a preview of the charges muckrakers like Phillips were to make two decades later: "The United States Senate is largely composed of rich men whose interests lie in preserving the dominance of corporations and monopolies." But the inclusion of Stanford would be a step down, for "among them all [there is] not one with so rascally a 'record' as his." Bierce pointed out that Stanford had begun work on the railroad as a relatively poor man, but that by letting contracts to himself—a felony under state law—he had become rich before even a single payload had been hauled. Stanford owed the government "of which he wishes to become a part" millions of dollars. He also had charged extortionary rates and fares, intimidated merchants, made false promises to property buyers like those at Mussel Slough, and corrupted politics, law, and business. Rather than putting him in the "hauls of Congress," Stanford's repeated flouting of the law should have earned him a place in another federal institution— a penitentiary.[37]

Given the complacent and even craven reaction to the Big Four by the California press, Bierce did not show much faith in its ability to rectify matters. The editorials noted the railroad's manipulation and outright purchase of other newspapers, as when railroad interests bought the struggling *Alta California*.[38] Bierce claimed he knew the railroad's tactics from private as well as public experience. In one editorial he reported that a person connected with the railroad had sent the *Wasp* a letter asking "the market price of our favor." His answer was to demand the railroad pay the federal government all money due "to the last penny," pay all state and local taxes without litigation, abolish rebates for favored companies, end subsidies of newspapers and government officials, and "most important," accede to a schedule of rates to be set by the state railroad commissioner.[39]

Though Bierce devoted much space to attacking the local press for its subservience to the railroad and for myriad other matters, his tone concerning the national press tended to be more respectful. Once he quoted at length an article in the *North American Review*—the magazine that had sponsored the Erie Railroad exposures written by the "grandfather of muckraking" in 1869—detailing various railroad land grabs across the nation.[40] Later, he tried to spur local resistance to the Central Pacific by pointing out that newspapers across the country were exposing railroad abuses and likening their efforts to "revelation of burglar-work by the intelligent beam of a bull's-eye lantern."[41]

Though his outlook was not optimistic, it was not completely pessimistic. Intelligence and truthfulness could change things for the better; resistance could be mounted to overcome even as powerful a force as the Octopus. But Bierce's time on the *Wasp* was running out, and by the middle of 1885, he no longer appears to have been writing the editorials. Items began to refer to Stanford's educational bequests, for instance, as "kingly," a type of obsequious description to which Bierce would never have assented, especially in connection with Stanford.

Not only was Bierce's hope for the awakening of an intelligent local press dashed, but he was slowly being squeezed out of the *Wasp*. He had never been a typical journalist or editor—although he wrote for San Francisco publications, he did nearly all his work from places outside San Francisco because of his asthma. By the middle of 1886, he was at an even further remove, again out of a job as the *Wasp* traded in biting wit for a kindlier, duller brand of humor.

Although Bierce had launched devastating attacks on the railroad villains, he had not been uniformly hostile to all parties. He had, for instance, shown compassion for a number of victims of the railroad and concern that the associates' ways had corrupted California's political system beyond belief and almost beyond repair. Bierce's journalism had advanced significantly as he moved from the *Argonaut* to the *Wasp*. He had freed himself from the fetters of Pixley's incestuous relationship with the railroad and enjoyed practical editorial autonomy during most of his tenure at the *Wasp*, when he fired his first steady volleys at the railroad. Changing times and a change in jobs had made this new and ferocious line of attack possible. The railroad had fallen in public favor. The tone also arose from Bierce's own indignation over his treatment by Pixley. As Bierce's repeated attacks on the cozy relationship between the railroad and the press suggest, he was only too glad to be free of that control.

His outbursts were muffled by the sale of the *Wasp*, however. "Freedom of the press in Britain is freedom to print such of the proprietor's prejudices as the advertisers don't object to," Hannen Swaffler observed in 1928 (and A. J. Liebling echoed in the *New Yorker* in 1960). Things were not much different in the United States in the nineteenth century. Bierce had learned this lesson well. But he was to witness it in a subtler and more ironic form when he went to work for the new owner of the *San Francisco Examiner*, the dynamic and enigmatic William R. Hearst. The wealthy young publisher, antagonistic to the railroad, gave Bierce the financial security that allowed him to attack the railroad. But the motivation for Hearst's antagonism to the railroad resulted at least in part from his desire to please the masses, thereby solidifying his newspaper empire and furthering his own political aspirations. Under Hearst, Bierce was to become disillusioned with muckraking itself. There was nothing pure about it.

NOTES

1. *Argonaut*, 14 July 1877, 5.

2. *Argonaut*, 22 December 1877, 5.

3. *Argonaut*, 18 May 1878, 9; 23 August 1877, 5.

4. John P. Young, *Journalism in California* (San Francisco: Chronicle Publishing Co., 1915), 104.

5. *Argonaut*, 2 January 1878, 9.

6. *Argonaut*, 2 February 1878, 9.

7. Carey McWilliams, *Ambrose Bierce: A Biography* (New York: Albert & Charles Boni, 1929), 122.

8. Jerome Hart, *In Our Second Century* (San Francisco: The Pioneer Press, 1931), 122.

9. Ibid., 156.

10. Richard Saunders, *Ambrose Bierce: The Making of a Misanthrope* (San Francisco: Chronicle Books, 1985), 36–37.

11. Kenneth M. Johnson, *The Sting of the Wasp* (San Francisco: The Book Club of California, 1967), 1–4.

12. *Wasp*, 11 September 1886, 4.

13. His near-total authorship of editorial content has been noted by Franklin Walker, *Ambrose Bierce: The Wickedest Man in San Francisco* (San Francisco: The Colt Press, 1941), 13, among others.

14. *Wasp*, 2 February 1885, 5.

15. *Wasp*, 5 July 1882, 5.

16. *Wasp*, 8 December 1883, 5.

17. *Wasp*, 22 November 1884, 5.

18. *Wasp*, 3 May 1884, 5.

19. *Wasp*, 21 March 1885, 5.

20. *Wasp*, 9 September 1883, 5.

21. *Wasp*, 2 February 1884, 6.

22. *Wasp*, 1 January 1885, 6.

23. *Wasp*, 2 September 1882, 6.

24. *Wasp*, 18 October 1884, 4.

25. *Wasp*, 24 January 1885, 4.

26. *Wasp*, 11 April 1885, 4.

27. *Wasp*, 27 June 1885, 5.

28. *Wasp*, 3 May 1884, 4.

29. *Wasp*, 27 October 1883, 4; 27 December 1884, 4; 17 January 1885, 4.

30. *Wasp*, 2 September 1882, 4.

31. *Wasp*, 13 September 1884, 4.

32. *Wasp*, 26 January 1884, 4.

33. *Wasp*, 20 December 1884, 4.

34. *Wasp*, 10 November 1883, 4; 17 November 1883, 4; 1 March 1884, 4.

35. *Wasp*, 9 August 1884, 4.

36. *Wasp*, 1 December 1883, 4.

37. *Wasp*, 10 January 1885, 4.

38. *Wasp*, 22 September 1883, 4.
39. *Wasp*, 14 July 1883, 4.
40. "America for American Railroads," *Wasp*, 10 March 1883, 12.
41. *Wasp*, 2 February 1884, 4.

7

Early Years at the *San Francisco Examiner*

William Randolph Hearst undoubdtedly hired Bierce as a writer for the *San Francisco Examiner* because he admired Bierce's wit and ability. Although the two men launched a powerful attack against the railroad, it is less clear that Hearst sought out Bierce specifically because of this shared antagonism.

Although opposition to the railroad was a mutual cause, the attack against the common enemy eventually helped alienate Bierce from Hearst. More exactly, Bierce became dissatisfied with the Hearst organization. In the few reflections he later left on his former boss, Bierce was always reluctant to criticize Hearst personally.

For Hearst, influenced by Pulitzer and his father, George Hearst, a United States senator representing California from 1886 to 1891, the fight became mainly a matter of building newspaper circulation and forging his own political opportunities rather than the personal and moral crusade it was for Bierce. Bierce did not explicitly complain of this. Like many employees of Hearst, he sometimes admired his boss and often was confused by his complex and contradictory personality. Bierce's repeated threats to quit the Hearst organization from the middle of the 1890s on, however, suggest he had had enough. Hearst's ambitions really began to become apparent in 1895, when he bought the *New York Journal*, and in 1896, when he dispatched Bierce to Washington to cover the Congressional wrangle over repayment of the huge debts the railroad owed the federal government.

For Bierce, the Eastern campaign must have robbed the cause of some of its purity. He had always been, to some extent, a Hearst hireling. But as a columnist for "Prattle," he maintained a somewhat distant relation with Hearst and his organization. When Bierce journeyed to Washington, however, he went to some degree as a hired gun. And he practiced a kind of journalism that was highly unusual for him, something approaching the shrill and gaudy reporting that decorated the front pages of Hearst's newspapers. For the first time, Bierce's writing appeared under big headlines on the front page.

The stunts and sometimes deceitful reporting methods that Hearst's men practiced and the demagoguery in which Hearst seemed to indulge himself became all too apparent as the 1890s rolled on. Bierce finally had found a publisher who had nearly unlimited financial strength and whose position on the railroad meshed with his. But he may have detected a small note of irony in his answered prayers as he gradually became disillusioned with the organization's methods and with his boss's reasons for carrying on the attack.

From 1887 to 1895, Bierce continued "Prattle" in the *Examiner*. In 1896, a landmark year not only in his tempestuous relationship with the railroad but with journalism, he suspended the column to take part in the funding bill fight in Washington. Until 1895, "Prattle," though true to its original form dating back to *Argonaut* days, changed in content. Entries became longer and more serious in tone. Bierce continued to attack the railroad and corrupt newspapers and politicians with his usual corrosive wit. But he began to write longer segments exploring the social and political character of the railroad problem, which by then had stagnated for nearly two decades. With a new spirit of opposition among San Francisco merchants jelling in the 1890s, he began to push for a revolt against the Octopus.

WILLIAM R. HEARST

Bierce languished for a while after leaving the suddenly stingerless *Wasp*. In 1887, the year after his departure, he was approached by young William R. Hearst, who had convinced his millionaire father to hand over the *San Francisco Examiner* to him.

Any observer who expected the paper to become a rich boy's plaything, to be used and then tossed aside, was disappointed. Before his expulsion from Harvard, Hearst had paid closer attention to the technique of exposure and sensationalism successfully employed by Joseph Pulitzer and his *New York World* than to his professors' lectures. Back in San Francisco, fresh with cash and ideas, he set about revamping the worn-out Democratic rag, later remembered by one San Francisco news-man as "one of the world's worst newspapers." It had "practically no circulation, no advertising, no talent on the staff."[1]

Declaring that "there is no substitute for circulation," Hearst set about luring customers by turning the hidebound journal on its head.[2] He hired new writers, began assigning reporters to Pulitzer-style inves-tigations and escapades, and engineered a good deal of circulation-boost-ing gimmickry—getting employees to rescue fishermen from a rock at the entrance to the San Francisco Bay, for example, or having a grizzly bear captured and brought to the city as the *Examiner's* mascot.

Bierce later related his own offer of employment in a possibly apocryphal vein. Hearst, he said, had come to his apartment personally and, in his strangely high and soft manner of speaking, offered him a job "in a voice like the fragrance of violets made audible." As a former business manager of the *Harvard Lampoon*, Hearst keenly admired Bierce's satiric talents.[3]

The circulation-building strategy worked. Despite a crowded field—six other newspapers competed with Hearst in San Francisco when he took over the *Examiner* in 1887—readership grew quickly. One esti-mate has it rising by as much as 1,000 a week at the beginning, a mag-nificent figure compared to the stagnant number of 23,914 claimed un-der its former, doddering editorship. Much of the old regime's stated circulation had consisted of party-subsidized giveaways, an attempt at bolstering the fortunes of Democatic candidates.[4] By 1896, the *Examiner's* circulation had surpassed that of its most formidable rival, the *Chronicle*.[5]

INCREASING OPPOSITION TO THE RAILROAD

The railroad changed during the 1890s, too. In 1893, Stanford died, leaving Huntington as the sole surviving member of the Big Four (Hopkins and Crocker had died in 1887 and 1888 respectively) and the undisputed dominating force driving the enterprise. Despite the severe depression that gripped the country from 1893 to 1896, the Southern Pacific corporation continued to roll up profits. It was one of the few large railroads, in fact, that did not become insolvent during those diffi-cult economic times.

The day of paying back the original thirty-year bonds obtained from the federal government was fast approaching, however, and it was becoming more and more apparent that something needed to be done, since the railroad had been neglecting principal and interest payments for many years. Though discussed publicly for more than a decade, the matter remained open. In 1879, Congress had passed the Thurman Act to augment an existing sinking fund that had been intended to pay off the debt out of the railroad's earnings. Less money had gone into the fund than had been anticipated, however, and the measure failed to rectify the deficit.

Political activity began in earnest in the 1890s as the possibility of foreclosure loomed. In 1894, Congress considered a refunding scheme called the Reilly Bill, but did not adopt it. Further proposals followed in 1896 but were not approved. This attempt at addressing the debt problem was commonly known as the funding bill and provided the subject matter for Bierce's scathing series of reports that many biographers have credited with defeating the measure.

Public opposition to the railroad continued to increase in the century's last decade. In 1891, a group of San Francisco merchants formed an anti-railroad organization called the Traffic Association and vigorously lobbied against the railroad, complaining mainly of unfair rates. The high, often uneven charges threatened the San Franciscans' position as the state's dominant jobbers; they feared their city would lose its prominence as a commercial hub. The Association became a major political force in the state as well as the city and helped elect a Populist, anti-railroad mayor in San Francisco in 1894.

So unpopular was the railroad that, in 1892, a pair of train robbers named Chris Evans and John Sontag became folk heroes of a sort after they held up a Southern Pacific express train in the San Joaquin Valley and made off with three sacks of gold. Henry "Petey" Bigelow, an *Examiner* reporter best known for his elegant attire and for a certain insouciance—he is reported one day to have suddenly announced to coworkers that he had tired of newspaper drudgery, and to have left immediately for Europe, not to return for a year—tracked the pair down to their lair in the mountains above Fresno. He soon returned, uncharacteristically whiskered, dirty, and bedraggled, with a sympathetic story to the effect that the robberies had been justified. The men were reputable farmers who had been robbed of the fruits of their labor by unfair railroad rates. It had been "rude justice" to return the favor. (Bigelow's sympathy counted little with a judge who, after the men were captured a few months later, sentenced them to twenty years in prison.)[6]

During this time, Hearst began filling his newspaper with anti-railroad stories. Though his father had been a long-time friend of Stanford, George Hearst had been supported for appointment to the

United States Senate by a Democratic machine that, like its Republican counterpart, was under the railroad's influence.[7] Perhaps the younger Hearst's anti-railroad campaign was in part a sign of rebellion from a leader of a rising generation. One historian, after all, has classified George Hearst as "a 'robber baron' of his day."[8] Perhaps William R. Hearst genuinely opposed the railroad's methods, or perhaps he merely saw a prolonged attack as a way of boosting circulation.

Train accidents got front-page play and columns of gory detail. Meetings of groups like the Traffic Association received much space. In 1894, the *Examiner* circulated an anti-railroad petition demanding foreclosure and a government takeover of the railroad. It got thousands of signatures.

Hearst's motives in making the attack may be debated. But he had found an issue that could stimulate the public. The railroad by this time had become very unpopular, especially in San Francisco, despite the efforts of railroad publicists like Mills and others, whom Bierce liked to lump together under the heading of "Huntington's literary bureau." Unlike Kearney's mob protests of the 1870s, the new backlash enjoyed the support and clout of wealthier citizens.

Although they made inroads with San Francisco newspapers like the *Call* and the *Bulletin*, the railroad's methods of buying editors' good offices through offers of advertising, free passes, and outright bribery had been more successful with small, rural papers, probably because they needed the money more—a weakness from which Hearst was immune. The *Examiner* continued to lose money even as circulation increased,but he had plenty of backing from his doting mother and somewhat more doubtful father, and was confident—and rightly so—that his investment in circulation would pay off in the long run.

"PRATTLE": 1887–1895

Bierce's attacks on the railroad from his new position on the *Examiner's* editorial page from 1887 to 1895 were similar to the barbs he had fired from the *Wasp*. If anything, they were less pointed and less frequent. He mentioned the railroad only twenty-three times in a little more than eight years.

In some years, such as 1893, his columns completely ignored the railroad or its principals. In most years, only a couple of items appeared. The highest number came in 1895, when he addressed the railroad eight times—still a small number, considering that "Prattle" was published weekly and that each column contained several items. That year's activity is probably explained by the new nadir of unpopularity the railroad had reached. The national depression had lingered, making rich men suspect in the eyes of many. Also, a good deal of adverse publicity had been generated by the railroad's efforts to avoid or delay payment of the government debt as the final payback date loomed closer.

In tone, too, Bierce's early work for the *Examiner* resembled the "Prattle" of the *Wasp*. His attacks against the railroad remained pithy, frontal, and personal, singling out Stanford or Huntington, the two surviving leaders of the corporation. Bierce's method did change slightly over the years, however. Until 1891, the targets of his jabs often included the sycophantic press alongside the railroad barons. From 1891 to 1895, he paid less attention to newspapers, and although he continued to attack Huntington personally, he began to pay more attention to social and economic issues.

His early attacks usually deflated the fawning praise and respectful quotes carried in newspapers when Huntington made his periodic visits to California and stopped to grant an interview or two. Frequently, these interviews avoided unpleasant questions about political corruption and instead investigated matters like the magnate's genealogy or his tips for getting on in the world. In one, for instance, Huntington is quoted as dating his family roots back to the Norman Conquest, but averring: "If I can't get glory for what I am myself I will go without glory." Beneath Huntington's quote, Bierce added a rhyme, which agreed that it mattered little to which "marauding race" Huntington traced his ancestry; "they're mostly dead," and thus could not "swear they've never cheated in their lives." Nor could they claim Loring Pickering and George K. Fitch, the owners of the *Call* and the *Bulletin*, two San Francisco newspapers in Huntington's keep.[9]

In another attack on newspapers' uncritical reporting of Huntington's pronouncements, Bierce exposed the corporate leader's apparently willful violation of the law of supply and demand. Huntington had stated in an interview that he favored consolidation of railroads on the theory that expenses would be lowered, and rates too. "What in the absence of competition would be the motive in reducing rates?" Bierce asked.[10]

In its very choice of language, the press was apt to be fawning, he noted. Bierce questioned newspapers' lip service to "republican tradition" after finding that "nine out of ten" had described Huntington's new mansion on Fifth Avenue as a "baronial castle." Bierce preferred to call it a "big new house."[11]

In 1891, Bierce's writing began to include more frequent mention of unfair rates. Fresno raisin growers had demanded lower freight rates but had been refused by the railroad, which pleaded poverty. The corporation's hard line was based on a lie. The railroad was profitable and Stanford was enjoying a magnificent property in Palo Alto while Huntingon was storming the gates of New York society. Bierce's response once again focused on individuals rather than on the corporate veil behind which they sought refuge: "Are their fine houses a dream, their vineyards and breeding farms and great business blocks, their United States bonds and banks and bank accounts a figment of the imagination?"[12]

Though he continued to attack the railroad, he conceded that its owners were unlikely candidates for reform. Learning that Southern Pacific conductors had been stealing train fares from the corporation, Bierce pointed out that they were only imitating management. The bosses might seek to stop the thefts by curtailing their own, thereby setting a better example. However, "accurately speaking, good example is not an infectious nor a contagious disorder—not, at least, without a longer exposure than is permitted by the rapidity of the disseminating patient's recovery—but perhaps by a special Providence it would in this instance be made so."[13]

In 1892, Bierce for the first time called for government takeover of the railroad. As a springboard for his suggestion, he cited a pamphlet, *Rescue the Republic*, by Thomas V. Cator, which pointed out the inevitable corruption by railroad interests of regulatory bodies like the Interstate Commerce Commission. The only real solution, according to Cator, was a government takeover.[14]

Bierce not only endorsed Cator's plea but called on the Traffic Association to distribute the pamphlet in the city. Further, he noted that although merchants complained of the railroad's tactics, they still dined and drank with the agents of the railroad's power. He urged the Association's members to snub the local, corrupt railroad commissioners, "rascals of magnitude."

In 1895, Bierce endorsed a mass meeting called by San Francisco's newly elected Populist mayor, Adolph Sutro, who was calling for Huntington's arrest. Bierce was ready not only for arrest but for conviction and punishment, declaring that "in the past twenty years there has been no day when he [Huntington] did not deserve to be hanged upon every limb of every tree of every acre of land which he has consecrated to his company's use by the laying on of hands."[15]

Although Bierce sympathized with such protests, his target was not great wealth per se, but dishonesty. He held "a rooted conviction that the penitentiary is a most suitable place for Mr. Huntington and his co-robbers of the Southern Pacific Company" and that the Standard Oil Company "by means of the power derived from its vast capital, has executed some singularly picturesque swindles," but it was "none the less interesting to estimate the total dishonest gains of the corner groceries."[16]

Bierce offered a theory to explain Huntington's seemingly limitless greed. It was, in his estimation, a thing that drove most men—"female admiration." Without it, he asked, "where would be Mr. Huntington's superiority to a pig with both forefeet in the trough?" The desire to impress women drove men to their ridiculous ends. Bierce concluded that "women's adoration, like a visible glory, follows and enfolds masculine distinction" and "powerfully affects the conduct of the ambitious," leading not only to colossal money grubbing but to lesser efforts like those of "Poet Waterhouse of Fresno [to] tear his ten thumbs to rags upon the lyre and execute memorable feats of mouth in subduing to song the disobedient voice long habited to invoking strayed swine to the evening meal."[17]

Bierce also continued to attack the railroad on the ground of safety, following the lead of the front-page articles in the *Examiner* that chronicled each new railroad mishap under big headlines. While the news articles picked over the grisly scenes for bloody corpses and shattered emotions, Bierce wrote of the railroad's dangers in a joking if macabre tone. Once he even proposed a serious solution. "Encouraged" by the railroad's apparent "suspension of total depravity" when it took upon itself the cost of adding electric headlights to its locomotives, he suggested "an electric uplight," a "powerful light directed straight upward," be added to each train. The device would reveal "to accustomed eyes the exact position of its train" and help prevent crashes.[18]

The journalist even took a turn at defending Huntington, although, characteristically, it was to attack another journalist. This time, he took issue with a report by Arthur McEwen, a reporter who had quit the Examiner to start his own sheet, *Arthur McEwen's Letter*, devoted mainly to criticizing Huntington. McEwen launched it twice, but its financing was wobbly—not surprising, given its opposition to the railroad—and each time it folded.

Bierce had supported McEwen's maverick efforts, but later assailed him, claiming he had used devious journalistic methods in the *Examiner* to smear the railroad man. By obtaining Huntington's letter to an engineer who had proposed a safety device, but by only partially quoting the letter, McEwen had tried to make it appear that Huntington heartlessly had refused to make safety improvements to the coupling devices on his freight cars. He had left out Huntington's statement that he would be "very glad" to get a new type of coupler that both worked well and protected human life.[19]

As the funding bill debate in Washington approached, Bierce again pointed to the difficulty of the political situation in California. The system had its limitations. Though railroad rates had been protested heartily for sixteen years, laws passed, and commissions set up, "all the power of a practically united public opinion, converging upon the [Railroad] Commission through every channel of authority, prescribing its duties and commanding their performance, making and unmaking its personnel, has, so far, failed to accomplish anything whatsoever."[20]

No easy answers presented themselves. The "customary moral" was that making the commissioners subject to removal at any time, rather than at the end of their four-year terms, would provide the solution. Bierce dissented, suggesting such a change would only make commissioners even more secretive, although "the experiment, doubtless, is worth making—along with those of proportional representation, the referendum, and whatever else naturally goes with it."[21]

For Bierce, however, all these progressive social prescriptions merely tried to hide the basic, irreducible flaw that was in man's nature. Worse, the democratic response of experimental methods might serve only to magnify that flaw:

We have now as good government as we deserve, and we are not likely to get any better by a new deal in methods. It cannot be too often repeated that in no country, in no age, under no system, has good government been known. . . . The immense majority of men and women of every race are fools and rascals: in that fact are to be found at once the necessity of government and the reason that it is silly and corrupt. The more power you give to this wrong-headed and wrong-hearted majority the worse will be the result. Individuals—even Presidents and Kings—are sometimes wise and good; the great body of the people, never.[22]

Bierce's "experimental methods" and "new deal" anticipated the Progressives and later reformers. Although he was willing to entertain such efforts, he lacked confidence in their success. Such attempts at righting wrongs were only worth a try. Given a corrupt human nature, they were unlikely to reap any real or permanent rewards. Like the muckrakers, he abhorred the abuses of the system. Like them, he advanced some suggestions for their correction—in fact, he went a good deal further than many of them in advocating government ownership of the railroad. But he was much less sanguine in anticipating victory.

The next year brought Bierce into his climactic struggle with Huntington. Though Bierce counted it as a victory for himself, it was at best a partial one. Widely celebrated at the time, its success in harnessing the railroad was limited. Publicly and privately, it was but a glancing blow, at most, to Huntington. At the same time, Bierce, the seeming victor, had become increasingly disillusioned not only with journalism in general but with his own journalism as he practiced it in the best of all possible worlds under Hearst.

NOTES

1. John Bruce, *Gaudy Century: The Story of San Francisco's Hundred Years of Robust Journalism* (New York: Random House, 1948), 201.

2. Ibid., 203.

3. Hearst was Bierce's last employer. The writer's work appeared in the *Examiner* and also in Hearst's *New York Journal* (its name later changed to the *New York American* after a quatrain by Bierce was blamed by some for the assassination of McKinley) until 1906, and in Hearst's *Cosmopolitan* until 1909. Tiring of newspaper work, Bierce repeatedly handed in his resignation, complaining of his editors' heavy-handed editing of his material and of the low quality of daily journalism in general. Always persuaded to change his mind. Bierce let his journalistic output decline in quality and quantity after the turn of the century. In 1900, the name of "Prattle" was changed to "The Passing Show," indicating perhaps a retreat from public affairs.

4. W. A. Swanberg, *Citizen Hearst* (New York: Charles Scribner's Sons, 1961), 41; Bruce, 203.

5. Janet M. Francendese, "Ambrose Bierce as Journalist" (Ph.D. dissertation, New York University, 1977), 31.

6. Edmond D. Coblenz, ed. *William Randolph Hearst: A Portrait in His Own Words* (New York: Simon and Schuster, 1952), 51–53.

7. W. A. Swanberg, *Citizen Hearst* (New York: Charles Scribner's Sons, 1961), 22–23.

8. Louis Filler, *The Muckrakers* (University Park: Pennsylvania State University Press, 1976), 130.

9. *Examiner*, 22 September 1889, 4.

10. *Examiner*, 26 October 1890, 4.

11. *Examiner*, 16 November 1890, 4.

12. *Examiner*, 14 June 1891, 4.

13. *Examiner*, 19 July 1891, 4.

14. *Examiner*, 29 May 1892, 6.

15. *Examiner*, 13 January 1895, 6.

16. *Examiner*, 9 June 1895, 6.

17. *Examiner*, 28 July 1895, 6.

18. *Examiner*, 4 August 1895, 6.

19. *Examiner*, 17 November 1895, 6.

20. *Examiner*, 15 December 1895, 6.

21. *Examiner*, 15 December 1895, 6.

22. *Examiner*, 15 December 1895, 6.

8

The Funding Bill and Beyond

Through 1895, Bierce remained in California, contributing "Prattle" to the *Examiner*. Early in 1896, however, his life and writing changed dramatically when Hearst sent him to Washington, D.C., to cover Huntington's attempts to convince Congress to cancel or delay repayment of the railroad's debts. The Washington trip resulted in an enormous increase in the number and the length of Bierce's writings on the railroad. For nearly four months, he poured out front-page articles for Hearst ridiculing Huntington and anyone who sided with him. He became, in essence, a daily reporter rather than the weekly columnist he had been for so long. The acidity of the language he used against the railroad and Huntington became even sharper.

Though still full of invective, his submissions resembled news articles more than editorials. In placement and layout they appeared as news, and also in style. Some included blow-by-blow descriptions of the proceedings. Meanwhile, his audience broadened as his work began to appear in Hearst's *New York Journal* as well as in the *Examiner* and as newspapers in Washington began to take notice of the struggle against the railroad.

Even as he was achieving what appeared to be his greatest journalistic success, Bierce was becoming even less enchanted with journalism. Certainly he had held reservations almost from the beginning. But his greatest newspaper success also became in a sense his greatest newspaper defeat, although the fault was not so much in Bierce as in the limitations of his craft. It was, after all, Hearst's fight as well as Bierce's. For the railroad forces, Hearst was the real adversary. They concerned themselves far more with Hearst than with Bierce, and they fought the publisher much more viciously than the reporter, attempting to smear not only Hearst's journalistic ethics but his personal life.

Hearst's style did not really bother Bierce. The journalist's written recollections of the publisher make it clear that Hearst perplexed him more than he annoyed him. But Bierce became increasingly irritated by the journalistic methods and motivations of the Hearst organization as a whole. Though there is no direct evidence of Bierce objecting to Hearst's yellow journalism per se, his increasing disgust with Hearst's editors and methods and his refusal to continue writing at times suggest that even as he was attacking the railroad, he was becoming suspicious of the motives for those attacks. As he recoiled from journalism, however, he produced some of the most effective and widely read newspaper work of his career.

Years earlier, he had tried to escape the field. Though he had been skeptical enough of newspapers to smite and lash offending reporters and editors ceaselessly, others remained whom he might "purify." But as the final decade of the century wore on, he began to sense that he was another sideshow in the circus run by Hearst and his subordinates. There was seldom any overt force or interference from Hearst, but Bierce was inextricably bound up in the cogs of the machine nevertheless. What had been a mission and a calling increasingly became just a job. Small wonder that a decade later in the new century, he would scoff at reformers and the muckraking scribes who supported them as demagogues and their flunkies who were advancing their various causes mainly to advance themselves and to fatten their wallets.

Although he was tiring of journalism, Bierce fired prose at Huntington that was strong, direct, and even gleeful, and he later claimed victory over the railroad man in personal terms. In terms of the public, the victory was short-lived and tenuous, a fact of which Bierce himself was well aware. Still, after the Washington fight, his mentions of the railroad fell dramatically. It was as if, having vanquished Huntington, he could leave the field.

BIERCE IN WASHINGTON

When the issue of repayment of the railroad's debt came to a head in 1896 and Bierce arrived in Washington to cover the funding bill fight, the railroad owed the federal government at least $59 million in principal and interest from the loans it had obtained in the 1860s. Because the government calculated the expected return at simple rather than compound interest and because of other easy terms, some observers have put the amount outstanding at a much higher level. These loans were scheduled to come due between 1895 and 1899.[1]

The railroad was seeking to avoid or at least put off repaying the loans, which had been made at six percent interest. Railroad lawyers and lobbyists advanced various schemes: cancellation of the loan, return to the government of some of the real estate obtained through grants, or payment of the old bonds with new bonds issued at a lower interest rate and a longer maturity. The last option was the most commonly discussed, and usually presented very easy terms for the railroad. One proposal called for paying the money back over a century at two percent interest.

Hearst devoted more attention to the funding bill than to the Reilly Bill, which the previous Congress had considered. Congressman James Reilly of Pennsylvania had proposed that the debt be paid back over seventy years at an even lower interest rate—one percent or even one-half percent per year.[2] Hearst had circulated a petition in protest and given the issue ample coverage, though not nearly as much as he afforded the funding bill in 1896. He had gathered, according to widely divergent estimates, anywhere from 19,663 to 200,000 signatures opposing the measure.[3] Whatever their number, they helped to sink the generous offer to the railroad.

Sending Bierce to Washington to cover the 1896 debate reflected Hearst's growing interest in running for political office. In 1895, he had bought the *New York Journal* from Albert Pulitzer, younger brother of Joseph. One of Hearst's trusted lieutenants, Sam S. Chamberlain, a former employee of James Gordon Bennett and of Joseph Pulitzer, had been sent East to manage the *Journal*. The hard-drinking Chamberlain, who had engineered many of the *Examiner's* news stunts in San Francisco, already had asked Bierce to come work for him in New York.[4] Though Bierce declined the offer, even his temporary presence in Washington would reinforce Hearst's eastern beachhead.

Bierce traveled east with his son Leigh in tow. He left Leigh in New York to learn newspaper work while he went on to Washington to report on the funding bill fight from temporary lodgings at the Hotel Page. From February to May of 1896, the *Examiner* published thirty-nine articles under his byline, all attacking the railroad. Bierce also contributed a number of unsigned editorials excoriating Huntington and his men during those months.

His journalistic methods during the funding bill fight were not in character with those he used at other times in his career. It was the only time in his life that he deigned to work as a mere reporter, to endure the give-and-take and the tedium of interviews and meetings and hearings, rather than to dispense judgments from columns he wrote at home. This new style of newspaper writing—for Bierce—was still very much a job, and perhaps even more so. He wrote his funding bill articles on rolls of brown wrapping paper, which he would tear off when he had produced the number of words requested by his editors. Occasionally, when he was angry at Hearst or the *Examiner*, he would stop filing stories, but he always resumed when his money got low.[5]

The articles were uncharacteristically long, in contrast to the one- and two-paragraph items that usually filled "Prattle." Frequently they reported Congressional hearings. Although they were factual, they could not be called "objective" by nearly any standard. They hit perceived villains directly and hard, while lauding perceived heroes and using loaded language to do so.

Telegrams from the Hearst offices in New York and San Francisco urged Bierce to interview certain persons, to get answers to specific queries involving the minutiae of the debate, and to keep up the attack. One dated 18 March, from an editor named H. Hamilton, directed him to "attend to C. P. Huntington some more" because "people seem to think we have quit on him." Other telegrams helped Bierce sort out the sometimes abstruse math of railroad and government finance.[6]

The articles often filled two, three, or more full-length columns in the *Examiner*. Many got front-page play. Assistants, reporters, and editors like T. T. Williams also contributed pieces on the debate, although they usually were supplementary to Bierce's. Often the words were accompanied by savage caricatures by Homer Davenport, himself a former brakeman for the Northern Pacific Railroad. Typically, these depicted Huntington as a fat, disheveled, cringing old thief.[7]

Though the form of Bierce's journalism changed markedly during the funding bill fight, the style of his writing did not. He continued to rely on satire, and usually aimed it at individuals. Since Huntington was the sole surviving member of the Big Four, he bore the brunt of Bierce's bludgeoning, although assorted aides and Congressmen also came in for dishonorable mention. Bierce often compared his satire to a hammer rather than a rapier, and his funding bill writing embodied that blunt style. Huntington, for instance, was said to have employed twenty-six lobbyists for the fight. Bierce relentlessly referred to the leading lobbyist, John Boyd, as "Huntington's tapeworm."

Bierce's opening salvo was purely personal invective, aimed largely at Huntington. Later in the fight he moved to a "blackmail" campaign seeking to discredit interviews with businessmen purportedly supporting the railroad. These had been published in the *Washington Post* by a Huntington agent, and Bierce, as he had for the previous fifteen years, fell to the task of exposing corrupt journalism and Huntington's encouragment of it. Later he devoted numerous articles to describing the public proceedings at the nation's capital, often portraying them as a corrupt, soporific, and absurd process. Many of these articles included lengthy descriptions of Huntington's testimony before Senate and House committees.

Even by late April, when it appeared the bill had no chance for passage, Bierce continued to hammer at another Huntington plan to get a federal subsidy to build a deep-water port at Santa Monica, California. Then, along with Congress and Huntington, Bierce adjourned for the summer. Following the struggle, both men became seriously ill. One historian, who has described Bierce's articles of the period as "models of scurrility," has suggested that Huntington's blurred speech during his testimony may have been the result of a stroke brought on by the journalist's unkindness.[8] In any event, both men soon recovered. Bierce resumed comment on the funding bill in the fall of 1896 and continued to mention it into the early part of 1897, though from the far remove of California, where he had resurrected "Prattle."

The funding bill itself faded away. Historians have agreed that during the emotional presidential election of 1896, which pitted William McKinley, Republican and friend of big business, against the Populist and Democrat William Jennings Bryan, Congress preferred to delay action on so controversial a matter till after the election. California would be a crucial state in that contest. When even the California state Republican convention failed to support the funding bill in June 1896, its chances for passage became nil.

Bierce had succeeded in helping to make the funding bill a matter of some national import, rather than a merely regional squabble. His invective and celebrity drew notice in the Washington papers. Meanwhile, copies of the *Examiner* were regularly given to congressmen and others in power. Ten thousand free copies of a special funding bill edition were issued to Washington's premiere hotels, including some that found their way to an unwelcome reception at Huntington's lodgings at the Normandie.

After McKinley's victory over Bryan in November 1896 (Hearst's *New York Journal* had been the only major Eastern paper to support

Bryan), foreclosure and the possibility of a forced sale or government ownership became unlikely. Congress considered the problem again in 1897, then took the path that elected officials often choose when confronted with a difficult issue. In July 1897 Congress appointed a three-member commission, consisting of the Attorney General and the Secretaries of the Treasury and the Interior, to study the matter and negotiate a solution.

As Stuart Daggett has pointed out, part of the government's predicament in resolving the issue was that it had placed itself in the dual role of both creditor and regulator. Any crackdown on rates would make it more difficult to pay off the loans. Thus the government's position was fundamentally at odds with that of the western merchants and farmers who desired lower rates. Ultimately, the government looked after its own interest. The eventual "repayment was not at the expense of the associates, but . . . represented merely a shifting of the burden of the debt due the federal authorities to the communities along the line."[9]

Early in 1899, the commission reached an agreement with the railroad's representatives. The debt would be liquidated in twenty installments over ten years at three percent interest. Unlike earlier laws and agreements, this one had teeth, and the debt was paid in a timely manner.[10] The loans that the railroad for twenty years had claimed it could not possibly repay were in fact liquidated without a hitch. The last payment came on 1 February 1909.[11]

THE FUNDING BILL ARTICLES

At the beginning of his Washington campaign, Bierce took pains to point out that most Easterners were unacquainted with the controversy, and he continued to attack California's corrupt press and the source of that corruption. The *San Francisco Evening Post* was perhaps the most extreme example. Controlled by the railroad, it was publishing dispatches purportedly written by Huntington. The *Post* once had been owned by Colonel Jackson, the same man who had bought and enfeebled the *Wasp*.

Huntington's side of the case consisted of several arguments: that the railroad did not have the money to pay the debt, that foreclosure would make rates even higher, and that a government takeover would create an inefficient railroad and soak the taxpayers. Bierce described Huntington as "the 'Post's' distinguished special correspondent, with one leg in the grave, one arm in the Treasury, and one eye on the police."[12] The journalist had a special bone to pick here, perhaps. One of his editors, Williams, was a former employee of the *Post* who had been forced off the paper for his criticism of the railroad.[13]

Seeking to take advantage of the nation's ignorance of the issues, Huntington and his associates began trying to prove to the Washington press and to Congress that Californians were firmly behind the funding bill. Mills instructed an underling named George Hazelton to interview scores of San Francisco businessmen to get statements in support of the railroad. Then, through unknown but probably corrupt means, Mills caused these to be published in the *Washington Post*, which did not then bask in the exalted journalistic reputation it occasionally enjoyed in the following century.

Bierce counterattacked, printing a "blacklist" in the *Examiner* of all the merchants quoted, claiming the interviews had been faked, and threatening to keep printing the list until each merchant renounced his support. There remains some question as to Bierce's claim. One letter, apparently from Williams, suggests that the statements were authentic. Referring to California businessmen as "dirty sneaking curs," the letter concedes that "though Hazelton is nine kinds of a son of a bitch I guess he quoted them correctly."[14] But the railroad was held in such low regard in San Francisco at the time that to have one's name connected with it was anathema. The businessmen quoted quickly began to recant when the articles were published in San Francisco. Bierce obligingly struck their names from the list as each sent in his clarifications and amplifications.

Bierce also exposed other efforts of the railroad to gather support. When corporate attorneys produced a witness representing the National Board of Trade to refute the complaints of the Traffic Association and to argue against foreclosure and government control, Bierce pointed out that none of the board's members was from California.[15]

Throughout, he kept up his personal attack on Huntington, "the arch malefactor and calumniator."[16] In his first article on the funding bill, he bludgeoned the railroad chief with escalating satire: "Mr. Huntington is not altogether bad. Though severe, he is merciful. He tempers invective with falsehood. He says ugly things of his enemy, but he has the tenderness to be careful that they are mostly lies."[17]

When Huntington later appeared before the Senate Committee on Pacific Railroads, Bierce ridiculed him as a dull and absurd coward: "It was plain that Mr. Huntington grew more and more nervous, and when at last he upheaved his bulbous bulk to address the committee, it was only to ask, in a half incoherent way, for more time."[18] Later, Bierce appeared satisfied that he had succeeded in wounding, humiliating, and vanquishing his personal foe. Reappearing before the Senate Committee, where he was grilled by the railroad's main opponent in the Senate, an Alabama Democrat and Confederate Civil War veteran named John Tyler Morgan, Huntington showed

every outward and visible sign of an inner torment that the flesh could denote, . . . pathetically defending his claim to the right of adding to his useless millions, shuffling, falsifying, cowering under the pitiless gaze of his persecutor, mortified by admissions already made and trembling under apprehension of ones to come. . . . Mr. Huntington is not the moral pachyderm that we Californians have always believed him to be. He feels the disgrace and discredit as keenly as anybody that cannot make up his mind not to deserve them. He sets as high a value on the respect and esteem of the reputable as he can afford to. He has more frank cynicism than he needs in his public business. No man need henceforth fear sharp words of censure will be wasted on this malefactor: they will not reform him. If not deterrent they will be punitive. The tradition of his invincible callousness is henceforth (to me at least) faded fiction.[19]

Though many San Francisco businessmen advocated regulation of the railroad's rates, they often stopped short of supporting a government takeover, fearing an expanded bureaucracy. Bierce went a step further than the merchants, however. Suggesting that it would do no good to extend a loan for another century to "professional defaulters" who had not paid back the original loan in a mere thirty years, he advocated foreclosure and government ownership of the railroad.[20] He pointed out that the Union Pacific and a number of other bankrupt railroads were being operated by receivers appointed by the government to represent the interests of creditors and that "we hear little complaint of selfish mismanagement." Should Huntington's railroad be operated for "the good of the whole people instead of a class," it could be reasonably assumed that its management would be even more equitable.[21]

The railroad forces soon counterattacked by accusing the *Examiner* of bearing a grudge about some advertising they had withdrawn. They claimed they had ordered thirty months of advertising with the *Examiner* at $1,000 a month, had paid for twenty-two months, and then pulled the advertising when Huntington became angry about some anti-railroad material in the paper's editorial columns. The *Examiner's* antagonism during the funding bill fight was caused by the cutoff, according to the railroad men, who set about widely publicizing the charge.

The evidence is equivocal. One study has shown that editorial space in the *Examiner* devoted to criticism of the railroad actually increased after the railroad started the advertising.[22] A tattered letter to Bierce from someone at the *Examiner*, probably Williams, makes this point as well, noting that despite the railroad's "patronage," the "'Examiner' was a[lw]ays jumping o[n] them. They tried in every possible wa[y] . . . [so?]me concessions from the 'Examiner' and failed."[23]

Huntington never made the allegation under oath. And though he accused the *Examiner* of being in the railroad's sway, he never made the accusation against Bierce. The journalist himself claimed that during the funding bill fight, Huntington once tried to bribe him and twice offered to shake his hand, but that he refused all the railroad man's advances. Significantly, Huntingon never publicly made the charge, later suggested by de Castro, that Bierce attacked the railroad because it had refused him a job.

As the negotiations and hearings dragged on, Bierce took the opportunity not only to attack railroad officials and politicians, but to refute their arguments and to support anti-railroad forces. He pointed out that the railroad's "poverty plea" was false, that the corporation had been making an ample profit, even during the depression, and that it could afford to pay its debt.[24] In fact, though the railroad did experience a drop in profits during the depression, it cleared $3.5 million in 1896 at a time when many other railroads were going bankrupt.[25]

Bierce occasionally described the entire legislative process as a sham. When Huntington appeared before a House committee, Bierce noted with mock astonishment that "when he had finished some members of the committee questioned him with a good deal of vigor. One would have thought they wanted to know something."[26] Though Bierce believed in March that the funding bill would pass, by April he had changed his mind. He credited himself and the *Examiner* with the reversal. The issue, he concluded, had been decided not by a democratic appeal to the masses and public opinion, but by focusing the attack by delivering copies of the *Examiner* throughout the fight to "every member of Congress, every head of a Government department, and every distinguished man in the service here."[27]

With the funding bill in abeyance, Bierce devoted a few more articles in May to attacking Huntington's scheme for getting a Congressional appropriation to build a deep-water port at Santa Monica rather than at San Pedro. Protected by palisades, the Santa Monica landing would have afforded the railroad a local monopoly. Bierce exposed Huntington's liberality in handing out free railroad passes while pushing for the bill, and pointed out that one senator owned 25,000 acres of land next to Santa Monica. Eventually the provision for the port was removed from the legislation.[28]

Though it has been claimed that Bierce was only negative in his life and journalism, he commented positively on both politicians and newspapers that sided with the anti-railroad contingent. He wrote glowingly, for instance, of Senator Morgan and of members of the House who opposed Huntington. After the *Washington Star* printed an interview with Bierce and took an anti-railroad stance, he called it "one of the great journals of the country." Bierce had met with the *Star's* editor and principal owner, Crosby S. Noyes, who had been reading the *Examiner* and promised Bierce his support.[29]

RETURN FROM THE "HAULS OF CONGRESS"

There was a hiatus for most of the summer as Congress adjourned and Huntington and Bierce recuperated. From August to the end of the year, Bierce, who returned to California in November, mentioned the railroad only three times. He was again writing "Prattle," and the style and subject matter returned to the norm of previous years. Occasionally he flicked small barbs at the railroad.

One spoofed the ghoulishness and pat generalizations of statisticians, who were quick to claim after every new train wreck that railroads were relatively safe. Bierce seized the opportunity to question both the safety of the railroads and the usefulness of statistics to those who become statistics. He doubted the statisticians' optimistic tone but agreed that "he that has the advantage of being in a smash-up, a part of the thing smashed up—who is roasted, boiled, skewered, or minced (and the methods are so various that all may be suited)—seldom dies of consumption, or even of senility."[30]

Later, he pondered the disproportionate reactions of individuals to public wrongs and to personal annoyances and the "superior intolerableness of a small wrong to a great one." Despite decades of outcry over the railroad's corrupt domination of California, members of the public seemed more aggrieved at seeing their own "trunks cascaded from a car and lost in a spray of their own splinters" than at the railroad's "bribery and corruption, their unspeakable steals of property and privileges, their dishonorable manipulations of the stock market, their defiance of the laws." Self-interest, usually unenlightened, ruled the public's brief attention span.[31]

In 1897, Bierce continued in his old style, occasionally mentioning the railroad in small items in "Prattle." After the tense and hard struggles in Washington, he mentioned the railroad only six times, mainly in the first few months of the year, when Congress took up the funding bill again. There now appeared to be little chance of passage and Bierce remained in California.

He was content in "Prattle" merely to reiterate his support for government ownership. For political reasons, however, he did not believe the matter should be pushed because the hobgoblin of a government takeover might actually help the funding bill. Government ownership would be "a beneficent extension of that true socialism in which we owe all that is best in our political system." But since socialism was used in the East "to frighten naughty children and blast the reputations of mature offenders," railroad opponents in the West should settle merely for defeating the funding bill and not dwell on the issue of public ownership.[32]

Later he went on to settle scores with old political enemies like Grove Johnson, the railroad's most stalwart political advocate, who shortly after the funding bill debate had been defeated in his quest for reelection to Congress. Bierce devoted the bulk of one column to repeating the discovery that as a young man, "Grove the Unspeakable" had forged another man's name to a promissory note. Subsequently the lawyer had been forced to flee New York to escape imprisonment for the crime.[33] Bierce also returned to his pastime of attacking California newspapers for their obedience to the railroad—specifically his old enemy, Jerome Hart of the *Argonaut*.[34]

Bierce's opinion of the winding down of the funding bill fight was typically ambivalent. Though pessmistic, he appeared to think the fight had been worth making. Undoubtedly he was worried to some extent that he had been a mere pawn in the game of Hearst's political ambitions and his editors' career ambitions. Letters to him during the funding bill debate, probably written by Williams, acknowledge Bierce's disgust at the methods of the *Examiner* and the *Journal*, which apparently included pilfering politicians' papers. Bierce himself was not accused of any devious methods.[35]

Still, publicly, Bierce concluded that though the railroad problem was far from solved, the defeat of the funding bill had been "an enormously long stride toward the open," and that celebration indeed was warranted. He also noted the eagerness of California's United States senators (Stephen M. White, Democrat from Los Angeles, and George C. Perkins, an Oakland Republican who had been appointed to replace Stanford after the latter's death) to take credit for the defeat after the fact, though neither "had at any time been an opponent of the funding bill."[36]

FIN DE SIÈCLE BIERCE

After a flurry of mentions of the railroad in the first four months of 1897, all concerning the funding bill, Bierce turned his attention elsewhere. During the next few years he spent much of his time tilting at a new and bigger windmill, and one that his employer adamantly admired: the Spanish-American War. Bierce, fully aware of war's chaos and absurdity but not a pacifist, opposed this particular engagement. Possibly, resentment that he had been a pawn of the Hearst organization during the funding bill fight contributed to his rebellion against his boss on the war issue.[37]

As a new century approached, a certain resignation and regret was abroad in the land. Bierce's friend Sterling became "sad without cause," reflecting "the prevailing end-of-the-century pessimism." The literati were "asking each other if life was worth living and writing essays about it."[38] Henry Adams, "drifting in the dead-water of the fin-de-siècle," reported that "not a breath stirred the idle air of education or fretted the mental torpor of self content," and looked inward.[39]

But a kind of desperate optimism existed, too. Here was an opportunity "to settle the age's conflicting issues before time runs out."[40] B. O. Flower predicted hopefully in the *Arena* that "the closing years of this century will be a grand climacteric period in the history of the world" and that there approached "in a very special sense a day of judgment."[41]

Though apparently little affected by the prospect of judgments, human or divine, Bierce did make changes in his life and work as the century ran out. In December 1899, he left California for good, taking up residence in Washington, D.C. In 1900, "Prattle" became "The Passing Show: A Record of Personal Opinion and Dissent." His newspaper contributions became less frequent and more diffuse as they spread to Hearst's Eastern papers, and his writing began to lose its punch.

Between April 1897 and the end of 1900, Bierce mentioned the railroad only three times. Once he pondered the mystery of human greed, and what drove men who were millionaires many times over to continue to pursue wealth with lies, bribes, and theft. Earlier he had decided women were the cause of Huntington's greed, as they were of most male ambition. But in 1897, he appeared less certain. In any event, that ambition was foolishly and pathetically in vain. Why had Crocker labored, even after becoming wealthy, "as slavishly, barring a few vacations, as does the clerk who apprehensively toils for a monthly compensation under $100," preferring "a life of toil and care" to living "in a natural and rational manner"? He could not understand it, Bierce admitted. He could only conclude that the supposed admiration for work was symptomatic of "coarse taste" and that the professed love of labor was a hollow attempt at concealing nothing more than avarice. Despite the praise of Crocker by most newspapers, which had "published column on column of eulogy," causing the people to line the streets "with uncovered heads to see his body borne to the grave," Bierce noted that the "futility of wealth to stay the Destroyer is matter for a just and generous indignation, a superior fury!"[42]

In 1899, Bierce devoted two paragraphs to celebrating the first of the railroad's payments to the federal government in settlement of its old debt. Bierce reminded Huntington in print that he had attempted to bribe him, and that Bierce had named his price as "the amount of your company's indebtedness to the Government," which "might be handed to my friend, the Treasurer of the United States." He finished with a punchline that had kept for nearly two decades: "Thank you, Mr. Huntington: it is a real pleasure to blackmail a gentleman so 'dead-easy' as you."[43]

Bierce's final attack on the railroad was similar to his early ones from the days at the *Wasp*—a personal jab, devoid of much social or political analysis: "The Rev. Dr. Talmage is pleased to ask: 'Is life sweet to you?' That depends, dear doctor, on whose life you mean. The life of C. P. Huntington, for example, is not sugared to my taste."[44]

Bierce did not have to endure that life much longer. Two weeks later, Huntington, seventy-nine years old, died unexpectedly at his lodge at Raquette Lake, New York, in the Adirondacks. Nearly every newspaper in the country cried out his death in large headlines. Though a few noted Huntington's career of bribery and theft, many described his life in laudatory terms. The slightly ambiguous memorial of the *Louisville* (Kentucky) *Courier-Journal* was only a trifle less adulatory than others: "His honesty was at least as good as that of the average man, and probably better."[45]

Although the *Examiner* took an ample if somewhat more acid part in the national outpouring, calling Huntington "one of the most notable figures in American life, whether one looked upon him as an agent of evil or good," Bierce said nothing.[46] His columns for the rest of the year contained no mention of Huntington or the railroad. Perhaps he considered Huntington vanquished after the funding bill fight. Indeed, the matter was very nearly over, although Bierce eventually did run contrary to the ancient Roman rule of speaking no ill of the dead. *The Devil's Dictionary* contains a backhanded memorial:

Loss, n. Privation of that which we had, or had not. Thus, in the latter sense, it is said of a defeated candidate that he 'lost his election' and of that eminent man, the poet Gilder, that he has 'lost his mind.' It is in the former and more legitimate sense, that the word is used in the famous epitaph:

> Here Huntington's ashes long have lain
> Whose loss is our own eternal gain,
> For while he exercised all his powers
> Whatever he gained, the loss was ours.[47]

NOTES

1. The amount, from Stuart Daggett, *Chapters on the History of the Southern Pacific* (New York: The Ronald Press Co., 1922), 393, is figured on the railroad's total debits minus $16 million in credits. A higher calculation of more than $100 million is suggested in an *Examiner* telegram to Bierce dated 4 April 1896.

2. Daggett, 395–398.

3. The higher figure is from Walton Bean and James J. Rawls, *California: An Interpretive History* (New York: McGraw-Hill Book Co., 1983), 200; the lower from Daggett, 404.

4. Letter of S. S. Chamberlain to Bierce, 1 November 1895, Green Library.

5. Lawrence I. Berkove, ed., *Skepticism and Dissent: Selected Journalism of Ambrose Bierce from 1898 to 1901* (Ann Arbor: Delmas Books, 1980), xxiii.

6. These telegrams, dated from February 1896 to May 1896, are in the Bierce collection at the Green Libary, and consist of messages from T. T. Williams, S. S. Chamberlain, and other Hearst editors.

7. In "Bierce, Hearst, and the 'Rail-Rogue' Battle" (unpublished faculty research project, Arizona State University, 1967), Ernest Jerome Hopkins includes only seventeen articles by Bierce during the funding bill fight. Many other *Examiner* articles are included without byline—save for one credited to T. T. Williams—and almost certainly are not by Bierce, but by other *Examiner* and *Journal* reporters.

8. David Lavender, *The Great Persuader* (Garden City, N.Y.: Doubleday & Co., 1970), 373, 427.

9. Daggett, 81, 425.

10. Lavender, 374–375.

11. Daggett, 423.

12. *Examiner*, 1 February 1896, 1.

13. Jerome A. Hart, *In Our Second Century* (San Francisco: The Pioneer Press, 1931), 92–93.

14. Letter with no signature from "The Examiner, San Francisco" to Bierce, 7 March 1896, Green Library.

15. *Examiner*, 18 February 1896, 1.

16. *Examiner*, 3 April 1896, 1.

17. *Examiner*, 2 February 1896, 1.

18. *Examiner*, 9 February 1896, 2.

19. *Examiner*, 18 February 1896, 2.

20. *Examiner*, 19 March 1896, 1.

21. *Examiner*, 9 February 1896, 2.

22. W. A. Swanberg, *Citizen Hearst* (New York: Charles Scribner's Sons, 1961), 98.

23. *Examiner* to Bierce, 23 March 1896, Green Library.

24. *Examiner*, 20 March 1896, 1.

25. Daggett, 364.

26. *Examiner*, 12 March 1896, 1.

27. *Examiner*, 22 April 1896, 1.

28. *Examiner*, 13 May 1896, 1.

29. *Examiner*, 20 February 1896, 1.

30. *Examiner*, 9 August 1896, 6.

31. *Examiner*, 27 September 1896, 6.

32. *Examiner*, 10 January 1897, 6.

33. *Examiner*, 17 January 1897, 6.

34. *Examiner*, 24 January 1897, 6.

35. T. T. Williams (?) to Bierce, 2 May 1896, Green Library.

36. *Examiner*, 14 February 1897, 6.

37. Many of these articles have been collected in Berkove's *Skepticism and Dissent.*

38. Joseph Noel, *Footloose in Arcadia* (New York: Carrick & Evans, 1940), 114.

39. Henry Adams, *The Education of Henry Adams* (Houghton Mifflin Co., 1918), 331.

40. Janet M. Francendese, "Ambrose Bierce as Journalist" (Ph.D. dissertation, New York University, 1977), 63–64.

41. Peter J. Frederick, *Knights of the Golden Rule: The Intellectual as Christian Social Reformer in the 1890s* (Lexington: University Press of Kentucky, 1976), 99.

42. *Examiner*, 25 July 1897, 6.

43. *Examiner*, 19 March 1899, 12.

44. *Examiner*, 5 August 1900, 24.

45. "A Captain of Industry," *Louisville Courier-Journal*, 16 August 1900, 1.

46. "Career of a Notable Figure in California's History," *San Francisco Examiner*, 14 August 1900, 1.

47. Ambrose Bierce, *The Devil's Dictionary* (New York: The Neale Publishing Co., 1911, reprint ed., Dover Publications, 1958), 81.

9

Railroad Reactions

Though Bierce claimed a personal victory over Huntington, if not an outright rout of the railroad itself, Huntington never anguished over his past behavior. If he felt some inner shame or remorse, he gave no outward signs indicating even a shred of psychic pain. Practically until the end of his days, in fact, he continued to declare that his actions had benefited not only the railroad but the entire state of California.

The railroad itself, despite the requirement that it pay back its old government debts, continued to benefit from its corrupt ways and high rates. As far as Bierce's only really tangible victory went—repayment of federal loans—the railroad's customers and new shareholders settled most of Huntington's ancient debts.

Bierce may have overestimated his own importance in the railroad's political constellation. Even during the heat of the funding bill battle, Huntington and his leading press agent seldom mentioned Bierce in letters they exchanged. They concerned themselves far more with the wealth and influence of Hearst and devoted a good deal of time and strategy to counterattacking his newspapers' assaults. They tried to do this by discrediting Hearst, not Bierce.

Even their concern about Hearst should not be overrated. Their loss in Washington, in fact, may have resulted in part from underestimating Hearst and his influence there. Doubtless, too, the defeat was in good part attributable to circumstances. The refunding was controversial. Congress had failed to pass the Reilly Bill two years earlier and there is no reason to believe it should have been any less reluctant during the extremely agitated presidential election year of 1896.

At the same time, Huntington and Mills smugly continued to assume they held nearly absolute control over the great majority of California newspapers, even as their political position in the state deteriorated. Probably they really did wield power over many of the state's newspapers, especially outside San Francisco. But they had perhaps indulged themselves in an overgenerous assumption of the power of the press to lead public opinion.

Even though Huntington had promised to reform the railroad following Stanford's death, the letters reveal that he and his agents continued to disburse subsidies, passes, and other bribes to influence politicians and newspaper editors. They used a variety of subtler methods as well.

THE HUNTINGTON-MILLS LETTERS

From 1878 to 1900, Huntington exchanged hundreds of letters with his press lieutenant in California, William H. Mills, who had come to work for Huntington in the 1870s. Not only did Mills direct the affairs of Huntington's Sacramento newspaper, the *Record-Union*, but he helped the railroad achieve its public relations agenda with the hundreds of California newspapers it did not own.

Mills accomplished his goals in a variety of ways: by distributing cash payments, sometimes in exchange for ads and sometimes not, by handing out free railroad passes, and by subtler means. He supplied smaller papers with articles friendly to the railroad. Harried editors often ran these verbatim, saving time and expense. He befriended some journalists and played upon his long acquaintance with other California newsmen. The Mills family and the Older family went on picnics together in the Oakland hills.

Mills's importance to the railroad organization is suggested not only by his frequent correspondence with Huntington but by a diagram of the seating arrangement at a corporate banquet for 109 diners on 5 May 1887. Huntington's chair is at the head of the horseshoe-shaped table. The seat to his right is marked for William F. Herrin, a powerful lawyer who was the railroad's top political operative in California. Mills's seat is next to Herrin's.

The Huntington-Mills letters are important for several reasons. They indicate the effectiveness of press attacks, especially those by the *Examiner* and Bierce. They show the railroad's methods of controlling the press and suggest the success of that control. They confirm, despite contentions to the contrary by some, that he and his agents bribed news-papers and politicians.

RAILROAD METHODS OF PRESS MANIPULATION

Though Huntington publicly denied any manipulation of the press, the letters between Mills and Huntington suggest otherwise. Mills attempted to mold a newspaper's stand by making appeals to reason or to personal friendship, by buying ads, or by distributing bribes in the form of cash or free passes. Occasionally he recommended that his boss buy a newspaper company outright to gain complete editorial control.

Mills often confidently assured his boss that he could have his agenda published as he wanted and that he could have railroad policies anointed by nearly all of the state's papers. For instance, in 1894, when Huntington was considering advocating a government takeover of the railroad, Mills suggested that he could easily convince papers to back this rather sudden and strange maneuver. Huntington's reason for mulling government ownership is not stated in the correspondence between the two men, though the likely explanation is that he feared he might be held personally liable for the corporation's huge debts. The railroad's opponents had hoped to saddle individual shareholders with the corporation's liabilities at one time, but that hope was dashed in 1896 by the United States Supreme Court.[1]

Mills wrote that he was on easy terms with the California press and assured Huntington: "I can readily have a number of strong papers advocate the idea. . . . There is scarcely a paper published in California outside of San Francisco which would take such a position unless they thought it would meet with the approval of this Company."[2] His confidence in his mastery of the press is evident in another letter to Huntington on a different matter: "I have never failed to accomplish anything I set out to accomplish with the press."[3]

The letters are filled with such optimistic assessments. Though his rosy judgments might be attributed to an employee's natural desire to impress his boss, it appears that Mills enjoyed a good deal of success in controlling California newspapers' coverage of the railroads. He held special sway over the rural newspapers, small, cash-hungry sheets that often were glad to accept the railroad's monetary inducements as well as free, professionally written copy. Fashioning this material so that it did not appear to be railroad boilerplate could be exacting and difficult work. Mills often complained of the task, but acknowledged he had to do it because the editors themselves were too inept to carry it out. Once during the funding bill debate, he promised to have a Grove Johnson speech defending the railroad published widely, but complained: "These country editors are willing to do something, but they do not know how to write and it is difficult to write the same matter over and over again without disclosing the authorship."[4]

Though Mills spent a good deal of time glad-handing editors and writers and entertaining them on their visits to San Francisco in his office at railroad headquarters at Fourth and Townsend, his methods also could be more direct. He listed the corporation's "newspaper vouchers" in 1896 as $54,805. The following year's vouchers, which he recorded as $35,296, no doubt declined because of the end of the funding bill imbroglio.[5]

Sometimes he advocated outright purchase of newspapers, repeating an old railroad tactic that had helped create the *Sacramento Record-Union*. Mills suggested buying the *Los Angeles Herald* or starting another paper in Los Angeles, but Huntington rejected the idea as an unnecessary expense because of Mills's mastery of the press.[6] Huntington also had considered buying the *San Francisco Call*, but settled for giving it monthly payments.[7]

The cheaper, easier, and more general method of harnessing the press, in fact, was in making direct cash payments to editors and publishers. Awareness of the corporation's bounty became so widespread, however, that both men complained of having to fend off editors wheedling for more. Seizing an opportunity, some became especially importune during the bitter funding bill fight. In August 1896, Mills entertained demands for $14,000 in "assistance" from newspapers in Grove Johnson's congressional district alone.[8] Bierce's ex-employer, the stalwartly Republican *Argonaut*, was proposing that the Republican state committee buy 10,000 copies at seven cents apiece for seven weeks and asking for another $12,000 from the Republican national committee. Other Republican papers were demanding an additional $30,000.[9]

Many editors had to weigh opposing sources of revenue, Mills realized: the direct cash payments of the corporation versus the more indirect but perhaps longer-term benefits of adding subscribers by opposing the railroad, which was becoming increasingly unpopular with the public. Editors knew that big circulations would eventually bring big money, not only in circulation revenues but in advertising income. This struck Mills as unfair, and in one note to Huntington his anti-democratic impulses resembled those of Bierce: "The temptation to cater to the prejudices of the masses—to do the thing which will please the greatest number is, therefore, seldom resisted in the publication of a news-paper."[10]

Occasionally the editorial requests became pathetic. For some time, Marshall Cushing, former editor of the defunct *Washington Capital*, had been dunning the railroad. Huntington's aides had been busily shooing away the former editor, who had laid siege to the Hotel Normandie, where Huntington was encamped during the funding bill fight. Cushing would send in his card five times a day, "making himself a most unmiti-gated nuisance to the hotel clerks by his insolent demands for an inter-view with Mr. Huntington," according to a Huntington aide, George E. Miles. Though Miles had explained to Cushing "at least twenty times" that Huntington would give him no money, Miles complained that "he sends in notes pleading terrible poverty and exposing himself as being on the eve of financial ruin—which appears to be the truth, for his pa-per has at last gone up."[11]

Politicians had to be accommodated, too. Grove Johnson, father of Hiram Johnson—Hiram fourteen years later would launch the most effective political attack against the railroad ever seen—was the only member of the California congressional delegation who dared to openly favor the railroad during the funding bill debate. Grove's support of the funding bill had been vigorous. Finally, incensed that it had not passed, he had delivered a scathing public attack on Hearst, intimating not too subtly that the newspaper magnate was a half-mad wastrel who suf-fered from a venereal disease he had picked up from various debaucher-ies enjoyed during his frequent world travels.

The railroad had got Grove Johnson elected, but during the fund-ing bill debate Johnson often complained to Huntington that he was not getting adequate coverage in his home district. Worried, Huntington fre-quently urged Mills to redouble his efforts to get good press for Johnson. Like Bierce, Huntington seemed to lay many of the world's problems to the male's desire for female approval, writing Mills: "I regret to see that he [Grove Johnson] feels a little depressed over the lack of support that comes from the California press. I surmise that the wives of different members save clippings about their husbands and so far certainly Mrs. Johnson has not acquired much of a scrap-book to hold the notices about her husband."[12]

Besides keeping loyal politicians happy with upbeat press clip-pings, Huntington also placated them with cash. During the height of the funding bill debate, he instructed a subordinate to give $10,000 to Senator Watson C. Squire, a Republican who had been Washington's first territorial governor (and who was defeated in his attempt to keep his seat in the U.S. Senate in the following term), "a most excellent friend of ours," noting marginally that the payment should be in "currency or else a cashier's check so that the bank will not know the money came from us."[13] This was some time after Huntington had publicly declared, after Stanford's demise in 1893, that he intended to get the railroad out of politics.

Huntington's keen business sense prevented him from taking one line of attack advocated by Mills. When the press man suggested that Hearst, Mayor Sutro, and the Spreckels family, sugar magnates who also opposed the Central Pacific, should be portrayed in the press as rich hypocrites stirring up the masses, Huntington demurred. His answer reflected practical as well as personal concerns: "I do not wish to attack the sugar trusts, as their leading man in New York, Mr. Searles, is a very able man and one of my best friends and, besides, we get a very large tonnage from them as they control nearly all the sugar of Louisiana."[14]

EFFECTS OF THE RAILROAD'S NEWSPAPER MANIPULATION

The most notable result of the railroad's press campaign was its lack of success in getting the funding bill passed during 1896 in spite of the corporation's wide control of California newspapers. Part of the problem was that the railroad enjoyed comparatively little influence with Eastern papers. However, the railroad's position also was deteriorating with the public in California despite its mastery of the press there. The press, as the muckrakers later learned, tended to follow rather than lead public opinion.

While Huntington continued to lull himself in the belief that the funding bill would pass, even after it was apparent to others that it would not, Mills threw up his hands in frustration near the end of 1896: "The newspapers do not appear to have any great influence, unless they happen to run on all fours with public sentiment. The newspapers in short do not appear to create public sentiment or produce results."

To prove the absence of the power of the press, he pointed out that McKinley had won the presidential balloting in San Francisco in 1896 by only 144 votes although he had been supported by four major newspapers there. Women's suffrage had been turned down overwhelmingly although not one newspaper in the state had dared oppose it. In the same election, Johnson lost his congressional seat by 5,000 votes in a district in which his fellow Republican, McKinley, won by several thousand.[15]

Despite Mills's gloomy assessment, he could take heart that public passions burned hotly but briefly. Two years later, despite the intense controversy over the funding bill, as well as years of newspaper reports on bribes, thefts, and other scandals concerning the railroad, he happily reported that the corporation had "defeated a communistic, Populistic legislature" and elected a governor, a board of Railroad Commissioners, and a Board of Equalization to its liking.[16]

If Huntington's "literary bureau" was not always as effective as its expenditures in time and effort might have made it seem, neither were press attacks on Huntington as devastating as they were sometimes supposed to be. In his letters, the man appeared as spiritually and financially impenetrable as ever, even at the height of Bierce and the *Examiner's* onslaught in 1896. Huntington repeatedly assured his press lieutenant that he took no umbrage at the assaults: "I certainly do not care anything about their [*Examiner's*] talk of me, for anything from their tongue cannot harm honest people; the only harm can come from praising them."[17] Several months earlier, he had written: "I do not care what they say about me, and if you should have anything you need not take any trouble to put me right as far as I am concerned. I do not trouble myself about what others think of me, as I only want to be sure that I think well of myself."[18]

A few years later, near the end of his life, Huntington still appeared unperturbed. In a twenty-four page letter to his Wall Street financier, James Speyer, he laid the blame for anger at the railroad to geographic, economic, and political jealousies and envy. In summing up his own performance, he claimed innocence:

As far as my part in the inception, construction, and operation of the Southern and Central Pacific Railroads is concerned, I am satisfied with what I have done. No man is perfect and the man does not live who can look back and say that he has made no mistakes, but the motives back of my actions have been honest ones and the results have redounded far more to the benefit of California than they have to my own.[19]

Though the *Examiner* frequently crops up in the Huntington-Mills letters, its place in the railroad's affairs could best be described as an annoyance rather than as a preoccupation. Usually, the two men discussed tactics for outflanking it in molding public opinion and seemed confident they could.

Bierce's name appears only once in the correspondence, and indirectly. It is possible he is mentioned in other letters outside the collection, or that Huntington spoke of him but did not commit his thoughts on Bierce to writing. But Bierce's practical invisibility in the correspondence suggests he was at best a minor irritant to Huntington, despite his description as a liberator by biographers and his own claim of having vanquished the railroad's leader.

Bierce's name is included in an unidentified newspaper article enclosed with a letter from Mills to Huntington. The clip, an editorial that counterattacked Bierce after he lampooned Grove Johnson as "Congressman Johnson from Dead Cow Canyon," apparently had been written by Mills. It probably appeared in the *Placerville Argus*, a small gold-country paper over which Mills had considerable control and which was in Johnson's congressional district.[20]

Though Bierce claimed to have humbled Huntington, Huntington's letters show that the railroad magnate was, at the very least, not willing to admit any shame. Though the letters may have been disingenuous, it is more likely that he was writing truthfully and that he felt no remorse. Huntington was not a sensitive soul. That kind of disposition would have been unusual in someone who had clawed his way up from impoverished origins. It is unlikely that he would brood for long over any kind of personal attack. Neither was the world in which he lived terribly ethical. If he had offered numerous bribes, they had never exceeded the demand. There had been numerous takers.

Huntington appears to have underestimated Hearst to some extent, perhaps hoping that he could outflank him by influencing newspapers and politicians in Washington. He also appears to have been overconfident of his position in the West. The letters show that he felt largely secure in his California stronghold, when in fact his support was crumbling. Years of economic depression there, and the gradual political organization of merchants and other railroad customers, had probably done as much as or more than the *Examiner's* attempts to shake that support.

The attacks of Bierce and the *Examiner* did serve as something more than an irritant, nevertheless. And they succeeded ultimately in the laudable though rather limited objective of getting the United States Treasury its money back. Nevertheless, since he bore no personal liability for the debts, Huntington was wounded much less severely than his corporation's ratepayers and new shareholders. Though the funding bill victory did reveal greater chinks in the railroad's armor, it was not so much a decisive turning point in the long fight against the Octopus as the continuation of a disjointed and piecemeal process that had been going on, to greater and lesser degrees, since the 1870s. Bierce and Hearst had won a rare victory, but it had been a defensive one—preventing the railroad from making another of its money grabs from the public trough. The anti-railroad forces did not muster a successful attack until more than a decade later.

NOTES

1. Stuart Daggett, *Chapters on the History of the Southern Pacific* (New York: The Ronald Press Co., 1922), 406.

2. Mills to Huntington, 2 October 1894.

3. Mills to Huntington, 6 May 1896.

4. Mills to Huntington, 20 April 1896.

5. Mills to Huntington, 31 December 1897.

6. Mills to Huntington, 3 October 1894; Huntington to Mills, 19 March 1896.

7. Mills to Huntington, 15 August 1894.

8. Mills to Huntington, 3 August 1896.

9. Mills to Huntington, 14 September 1896.

10. Mills to Huntington, 23 March 1896.

11. G. E. Miles to I. E. Gates, 27 May 1896.

12. Huntington to Mills, 3 April 1896.

13. Huntington to Gates, 7 April 1896.

14. Huntington to Mills, 4 April 1896.

15. Mills to Huntington, 5 November 1896.

16. Mills to Huntington, 9 November 1898.

17. Huntington to Mills, 28 April 1896.

18. Huntington to Mills, 12 January 1896.

19. Huntington to James Speyer, 6 December 1899.

20. Mills to Huntington, 20 April 1896.

10

Ministry of Light

BIERCE AND HIS JOURNALISM

"I exult with difficulty," Bierce is reported to have said when he learned of the funding bill settlement of July 1897.[1] That difficulty he did not make completely clear. Perhaps it lay in disappointment with the committee's compromise. He had supported a government takeover, after all. Perhaps it reflected his growing disenchantment with the "yellow" methods of Hearst and his editors. From the time of Hearst's purchase of the *New York Journal*, Bierce had stepped up his threats of resignation. In any event, his reluctant rejoicing could be assumed to represent his mixed opinion of the means and ends of his entire battle against the railroad.

The *Journal*, popularly referred to as "the chambermaid's own," had not risen much in literary esteem with its change in ownership. Hearst had embarked on a full-fledged circulation war in New York, adding even more sensationalism to the *Journal's* columns and dropping its price to a penny in an effort to overtake the *New York World*, idol of his college days. He had little monetary or political incentive to improve the paper's contents and was well aware that the most intellectual paper in the city, the *New York Evening Post*, had the lowest circulation.[2]

The railroad was not only a target but, in a less direct way, a source of the yellow journalism that Hearst helped create. In the latter sense, the railroad had sown the seeds of its own destruction. Railroads had opened up national markets and paved the way for advertising, shifting the economic basis of newspapers and magazines from political patronage to advertising dollars. To get advertisers, newspapers needed circulation. Thus was born yellow journalism, from the approbation of business managers like T. T. Williams who were "ripe and ready for any method which would serve to extend circulation and therefore make advertising space more valuable."[3] Corporations like the Southern Pacific, relying very much on the old system of political patronage, had become targets of Hearst's yellow journals. In like manner, muckraking national magazines like *Cosmopolitan* and *McClure's* became vehicles for national advertisers even as they attacked the railroads that moved their advertisers' products.[4]

Bierce had been ambivalent about journalism for a long time—for most of his career, in fact. In the beginning, his writing had indicated some hope of improvement through liberal applications of hellfire, but with gathering experience his ambivalence began to turn to hatred of newspapers and to displeasure with his own situation. His copy was manipulated by Hearst's flunkies and he recoiled from the stunts and fabrications of daily journalism. At the same time, it was a living—as much for Bierce as for the others.

In his early days, he had attacked journalism with a view to exposing and perhaps mending its ills, to "purifying" those worth saving. Now at best he looked upon it as a job. In 1899, he had complained in a letter to a friend that "Mr. Hearst lets his fools, fakers and freaks do what they would with it ["Prattle"] in the New York Journal—the which I could nowise abide. They yellowed it every way they knew how, and mangled it at will."[5] Some years later, he refused Hearst's plea that he attack Pulitzer: "I don't like the job of chained bulldog to be let loose only to tear the panties off the boys who throw rocks at you. You wouldn't like it yourself in my place. Henceforth I won't bite anybody, a quiet life for mine."[6]

Even before the funding bill fight, Bierce had taken a skeptical view of journalism's power for reform or for any end beyond mere commerce. In August 1892 he had written his friend Sterling:

You ask me of journalism. It is so low a thing that it may be legitimately used as a means of reform or a means of anything deemed worth accomplishing. It is not an art; art, except in the greatest moderation, is damaging to it. The man who can write well must not write as well as he can; the others may, of course. Journalism has many purposes, and the people's welfare *may* be one of them; though that is not the purpose—in chief, by much.[7]

Assuredly, Bierce considered his attacks on Huntington a personal victory. The later articles in his series on the funding bill fight depicted the railroad chief as a humiliated and broken man. His detailed description of Huntington's wretched physical appearance was meant to confirm that victory. By his own standards for satire and its uses, Bierce's journalistic campaign had been a success.

The Huntington-Mills letters make it clear at the same time that Huntington himself claimed to feel little or no humiliation. It is possible that he deceived himself or others in this case. Certainly he had lied quite freely about other matters, and he had more than the normal human capacity for self-deception. Even so, if Huntington did convince himself of his innocence, or if he simply went unscathed by Bierce's assaults, Bierce's victory was one-sided and incomplete. His formula for journalistic success counted on the victim cringing under the sting of his lashes.

PROGRESSIVE REFORMS

The railroad itself continued in much the same mode even after Huntington's death. His heirs sold it to E. H. Harriman, who joined it corporately with his Union Pacific Railroad, its logical Eastern connection. Thus the two roads that had raced through Utah after the Civil War to collect government subsidies were joined into one. The combined railroad thereupon became the biggest in the country, an agglutination that was to be attacked and forced asunder in 1913 under the Sherman Antitrust Act.[8]

According to all accounts, the western railroad's corrupt ways in California continued unabated through much of the first decade of the new century, despite the change in ownership. In fact, its chief political boss, Herrin, once declared that its power in the state increased after the turn of the century, more than twenty years of attacks by Bierce and others notwithstanding.[9]

Opposition continued to simmer. In 1906, President Theodore Roosevelt and Congress gave the Interstate Commerce Commission real power to regulate railroads under the Hepburn Act. Baker, following his muckraking series in *McClure's*, personally advised Roosevelt on the minutiae of railroad rates. In California soon after, the Lincoln-Roosevelt League, which had identified itself with the growing national Progressive movement, was also making inroads against the Southern Pacific. By 1907, some thirty California newspapers had pledged support to the League. Two years later, for the first time in memory, the legislature passed a railroad regulation bill "not entirely without teeth."[10]

In 1910, Hiram Johnson, son of the railroad's long-time political lackey, Grove, was elected governor of California on a Progressive platform. His primary mission was to rein in the railroad, and in that he succeeded better than anyone before him. Father and son had become estranged over the father's subservience to the machine, and Hiram's embarrassment over his father's servitude no doubt was a driving incentive for exacting retribution.

So intent was Hiram on curbing the railroad's power, in fact, that he had to be convinced by his advisers during the gubernatorial campaign to devote some attention to other Progressive issues such as establishing an initiative and a referendum and advocating women's rights and labor concerns. He was elected promising a showdown between "the great moral masses" and "the corrupt but powerful few."[11] Bierce's thoughts on Hiram's "moral masses" have not been recorded but could well be imagined.

A legislature was elected that swiftly passed Progressive measures intended to limit the railroad's power. Laws were passed in 1911 that regulated rates and set standards for service, safety, and accounting. Within a year, it was said, a new, more powerful railroad commission already had saved shippers and travelers more than two million dollars by ordering reduced rates. It had to be admitted, however, that the bulk of these savings went to large farmers and shippers. Despite the railroad's decades of protest that it was financially unable to reduce its rates, it continued to operate profitably.[12]

The new governor and legislature were, in fact, regulatory but not revolutionary. Unlike Bierce, and unlike socialist muckrakers such as Russell, they did not advocate a government takeover. Paradoxically, this moderate regulatory approach ultimately may have saved the railroad from such a stern measure. In any event, the railroad had finally been curtailed after nearly fifty years of stealing public money and buying California's politicians and newspapers. One of Hiram Johnson's biographers has credited him with California's "emancipation from railroad rule," describing it as his greatest achievement.[13]

Some have protested that the railroad continued to play an unduly important part in the state's affairs into the 1940s. This may be so, just as there is no gainsaying the fact that corporations and their lobbyists continue to play at least as important a part in politics today, though in subtler yet far grander ways than employed by Huntington and his men. The avowal of Huntington's right-hand man, Herrin, in 1913 that "no railroad manager would agree to dispense with government regulation at the cost of returning to the old conditions" suggests that a certain amount of skepticism of the new Progressive regime's effectiveness may indeed be in order.[14] At the same time, it cannot be said that the railroad's methods ever again approached the outrageous tactics employed during its first half-century of existence.

Bierce and Hiram Johnson were mutual friends of Sterling's uncle, F. C. Havens, sometimes called "the Piedmont Midas" for the millions he had made off Berkeley real estate and a Berkeley railway. In the summer of 1911, Noel has Bierce and Johnson sipping wine on the porch of Havens's summer cottage in Sag Harbor, Long Island.[15] It would be fascinating to learn of their discussion and whether they spoke of the funding bill fight, Hiram's father, Hiram's inroads against the railroad, and Progressive politics and muckraking in general. But that conversation, if it indeed took place, apparently has not been recorded.

BIERCE ON MUCKRAKING

Such tidbits as Bierce did leave concerning muckraking and reform in the early 1900s are few and not kind. Clearly, he wanted no truck with reformers or Progressives. Often, and true to form, he based his attacks on personal character. In one bit of doggerel, he ridiculed a muckraker personally while also suggesting he advocated a type of anarchy:

> 'I'm sorry I married,' says Upton Sinclair:
> 'The conjugal status is awful!—
> The devil's device, a delusion and snare.'
> Worse, far worse than that—it is lawful![16]

Bierce is known to have made only one other reference to muckrakers. It is provided by Noel, recounting a conversation he supposedly had with Bierce and Sterling in Carmel, California. Bierce is said to have disparaged David Graham Phillips and his muckraking of the United States Senate. For Bierce, according to Noel, the majority of senators were not corrupt but merely stupid, and Phillips was a hypocrite: if he "ever turned on himself the muckrake he was using for befouling the reputation of his betters, he would stir up much that would smell to heaven."[17]

Occasionally, Bierce attacked reform in his increasingly rare and listless contributions to *Cosmopolitan*, tacking in the opposite direction from the lengthy muckraking articles that were crowding around his tiny space in the magazine. He argued that poverty and inequality could never be abolished, despite the best of intentions. Man's mastery of technology might advance, but man's brutish nature would not improve much, and reform would in fact hasten the decline of civilization, such as it was.

Progress would make the country soft. Preventing war, disease, and famine would merely bring overpopulation, which would be corrected by war, disease, and famine: "Progress is infected with the germs of reversion: on the grave of the civilization of today will squat the barbarian of tomorrow. . . ."[18]

Francendese has suggested Bierce wrote such articles out of a desire to gain attention by dint of their very perversity. But it is more likely he was holding true to what he considered to be older principles—the cyclical concept of history held by Stoics like Marcus Aurelius, rather than the more whiggish and linear ideal of steady progress that muckrakers like Tarbell and Baker were likely to invoke during their muckraking years.[19] For the Stoics, there was nothing new under the sun. For the muckrakers, at least while they wrote their articles, positive change, albeit grindingly slow and frustrating, was likely and even inevitable.

Bierce's relations with the editors of the muckraking *Cosmopolitan* were even worse than his running battles with Hearst's newspaper editors. Still, in 1906, they managed to get him to participate in a roundtable discussion with two reformers, Robert Hunter, author of *Poverty*, and Morris Hillquit, author of *History of Socialism in the United States*. The impression left is of a bearbaiting, with the younger men verbally dancing around and jabbing at an elderly, cornered Bierce. The older journalist is cast as the out-of-step reactionary, and his dullness seems to set off the metallic brilliance and smug self-assurance of his two attackers, one of them described glibly in the magazine as a "scientific socialist."[20]

Though Hunter brought up the muckrakers during the conversation, pointing out that Phillips, Tarbell, Baker, and the rest were producing their articles because magazine editors were responding to a demand for such stuff, Hillquit cut in and changed the subject before Bierce could reply. Bierce held steady in his defense that poverty was an unavoidable societal ill, but that persons with brains could escape it. Perhaps with Huntington in mind, he pointed out that "three-fourths of the presidents of the railroads" were born in poverty. He took care to add that the accumulation of wealth was not a particularly noble or even interesting goal.[21]

Perhaps Bierce, as a muckraker emeritus, was put out at being assailed by a younger generation that seemed to have forgotten his former role. Referring to "that fool symposium" in a letter to Sterling, he later dismissed his adversaries in a line: "I don't argue with babes and sucklings."[22]

BIERCE AS MUCKRAKER

For all his antipathy to the muckrakers of the new century, Bierce had exhibited many of their traits while battling the railroad, especially during the funding bill fight. His problem, perhaps, was that he had preceded this new generation, and encountered certain difficulties that they had yet to see. In this, he had outdone many of the social reform journalists of his own era, going far beyond their often tepid pleas, half-baked investigations, and overreliance on words at the expense of action. When he came to view the "new journalism" of the twentieth-century muckrakers, he had not only the experience of the process, but also the greater knowledge that reform is not as easily attained as imagined, and its effects not so predictable.

Still, putting aside the classifications of time and medium, Bierce in many ways fit the standard definition of muckraking. He was intensely individualistic. His whole method of attack, in fact, revolved around individualism. He shared the Protestant, midwestern background common to the breed. Though he lacked a formal college education, the knowledge he gained from his uncle, his father, various mentors, and his own reading was at least as broad as that certified by a degree. His background might even be characterized as middle class, in breeding if not in economic circumstances, and in any event he attained that level of financial comfort through his work.

He shared the muckrakers' essential conservatism. The answer lay as much in enforcing existing laws as in making new ones. Though he occasionally paid small tribute to the problems labor suffered under the railroad, he was far more sympathetic to the difficulties of the merchant class, and mentioned unfair rates more often. It was the Traffic Association, the group organized by San Francisco merchants to fight Huntington, in fact, that became one of the *Examiner's* most powerful allies, and the merchants were major beneficiaries of the eventual reduction in rates brought about by a Progressive governor and legislature.

In the Big Four and especially in Huntington, Bierce found an ideal central villain around which he could build his muckraking narrative. Bierce's target, the marauding railroad, was a common one among the twentieth-century muckrakers. He did not attack it as a corporation, however, because he believed that term a mere construct. The word itself was simply a marker for an abstract aggregation. Humans, not abstractions, were susceptible to attack.

The topic was of wide scope—as important to the nation as many of the issues addressed in later muckraking articles. The funding bill debate ultimately made that clear when Bierce and the *Examiner* expanded the subject of the railroad's plundering ways from a regional controversy to a national one.

In effectiveness, Bierce's muckraking was less successful than that of later muckrakers. His journalistic thrusts led to no specific legislation, although they did succeed in helping to prevent legislation favorable to the railroad. But he did win a small battle in showing that the railroad could be successfully challenged, and he helped clear the way for later reforms. This is a considerable accomplishment because Bierce, though not exactly the lonely warrior depicted by some of his biographers, had not quite the widespread backing of the public enjoyed by later muckrakers, nor the comforting knowledge that hundreds of other journalists and many other periodicals were using similar means to advance more or less similar ends. In that sense, he was a scout, just as he had been at one time in the army. Although his fight had occasionally mirrored public concern, often it had been the public that had to catch up with him.

In two ways, at least, his aims and methods exceeded those of many later muckrakers. One was his call not only for regulation of the railroad but for government ownership. This went beyond anything ever advocated by Baker, though it was the preferred solution of a minority, including the socialistic Russell. Too, Bierce extended the literary devices of satire and of the central villain well beyond anything done by the muckrakers. Subtlety, in Bierce's hand, was a tool for art but not for journalism, and he bludgeoned Huntington and his cohorts cruelly. His satire was more brutal by far, and his villains more villainous.

Muckrakers sometimes gave the impression after coming away from an interview with a captain of industry that plundering on the grand scale was a corporate problem and not an individual responsibility. If President A were to be replaced by President B, the same temptations would likely snare him. For Bierce, there was no defense. The fault lay entirely in character. The only inference that could be drawn from widespread corruption was that human nature was corrupt. This conclusion certainly was not a great leap from the essential outlook of the Puritans or of the Stoics and Cynics.

The muckrakers tended to attack corporate power and its perceived evils. Bierce targeted individuals, the supply of which was endless. For every wicked man or woman Bierce might skewer with his pen—to his own satisfaction, at least—there remained a pool of millions from which replacements were certain to spring up. He himself had little faith in the possibility of reform, or in a utopian aftermath, but that did not stop him. In the case of railroads, though they were not the salvation that boosters and, to a lesser extent, reformers like his uncle had promised during Ambrose's youth, they might at least be run fairly, honestly, and efficiently.

In method, only Bierce's funding bill attacks could be called real muckraking, for, unlike "Prattle," they were more in the nature of reporting than editorial commentary. This is not to say that those articles were "objective" in the way the term is used today to discuss an ideal (and humanly unattainable) journalism. They were not. Had they been objective, even if that were possible, he surely would have accomplished even less.

Paradoxically, it was just at this time, as he was entering his real muckraking period, that he probably came to clearly understand the mixed motives and political demagoguery of his boss, which colored, to some extent, his own efforts. He was not just in Washington to smite the evildoers. His cause was not entirely pure. He was there to boost the circulation of Hearst's yellow journals and his political capital. For Bierce, journalism never had the purity of art. It always involved the compromises of life. It was muckraking in its original sense as well: a living, and an often dirty one. His muckraking "victory" and the celebratory parades back in San Francisco must have been bittersweet.

One must have illusions in order to become disillusioned. Bierce's retreat from his own was a long one. Perhaps he really had become violently disillusioned during the Civil War, as one "sharp break" theory suggests. More likely, the long and hard experience of life slowly eroded his ideals and at the same time reinforced the early hypotheses he formed based on the writings of men like Marcus Aurelius and Epictetus. He had tried to live as a Cynic, in the classical sense. It was not until the last few years of his life, complaining about money and embittered about his fleeting public success, that he could be called a cynic in the sense that it is commonly used today.

Like much else in Bierce's life, his muckraking had been an incomplete success, but a courageous and brilliant one nevertheless. He had not reformed Huntington, but he had shown him to the world and to his own satisfaction be a pious fraud. He had not defeated the railroad, but he had won a battle against great odds.

Bierce, a reluctant reformer, certainly had some appreciation of ironic twists, which he typically inflicted on his fictional characters. Perhaps he had his journalism in mind when he included the following lines in his *Collected Works*:

> The sea-bird speeding from the realm of night
> Dashed to death against the beacon-light.
> Learn from its evil fate, ambitious soul,
> The ministry of light is guide, not goal.[23]

According to a researcher who sought out Bierce's daughter in Los Angeles, Helen reported that her father had written a biography of Hearst, but stored the manuscript somewhere in Laredo, Texas, before he crossed the border into Mexico late in 1913. Such a manuscript has never surfaced, although a brief appraisal of Hearst is included in the *Collected Works*.[24]

If it ever did exist, a book-length biography might have revealed Bierce's conclusions about yellow journalism and muckraking. In any event, Bierce's answer to Baker's problem of "living in a crowded world" finally was to leave it.

NOTES

1. Paul Fatout, *Ambrose Bierce: The Devil's Lexicographer* (Norman: University of Oklahoma Press, 1951), 223.

2. W. A. Swanberg, *Citizen Hearst* (New York: Charles Scribner's Sons, 1961), 81.

3. Will Irwin, *The American Newspaper* (Ames: The Iowa State University Press, 1969), 14.

4. Theodore Peterson, *Magazines in the Twentieth Century* (Urbana: University of Illinois Press, 1964), 4.

5. Carey McWilliams, *Ambrose Bierce: A Biography* (New York: Albert & Charles Boni, 1929), 259.

6. Ibid., 295.

7. Bertha Clark Pope, ed., *The Letters of Ambrose Bierce* (San Francisco: The Book Club of California, 1922), 7.

8. Lloyd J. Mercer, *E. H. Harriman: Master Railroader* (Boston: Twayne Publishers, 1985), 86.

9. George E. Mowry, *The California Progressives* (Berkeley: University of California Press, 1951), 15.

10. Ibid., 70–81, 123.

11. Ibid., 120, 133.

12. Spencer C. Olin Jr., *California's Prodigal Sons: Hiram Johnson and the Progressives, 1911–1917* (Berkeley: University of California Press, 1968), 37–41.

13. Ibid., 171.

14. Ibid., 171.

15. Joseph Noel, *Footloose in Arcadia* (New York: Carrick & Evans, 1940), 122.

16. George Barkin, ed., *The Sardonic Humor of Ambrose Bierce* (New York: Dover Publications, 1963), 67.

17. Noel, 199

18. Ambrose Bierce, "If Reform Reformed," *Cosmopolitan*, 46 (December 1908): 1.

19. Janet M. Francendese, "Ambrose Bierce as Journalist" (Ph.D. dissertation, New York University, 1977), 211.

20. "The Social Unrest," *Cosmopolitan*, 44 (July 1906): 297–302.

21. Ibid., 298.

22. Pope, 124.

23. Ambrose Bierce, *The Collected Works of Ambrose Bierce* (New York: The Neale Publishing Co., 1909–1912), 8:374.

24. From Paul Jordan Smith's notes in the Bierce collection at Stanford.

Bibliography

Adams, Henry. *The Education of Henry Adams*. Boston: Houghton Mifflin Co., 1918.

"An Odd Preface." *Bookman*, 30 (October 1909): 120–125.

Baker, Ray Stannard. *American Chronicle: The Autobiography of Ray Stannard Baker*. New York: Charles Scribner's Sons, 1945.

_____. "Railroads on Trial." *McClure's*, 25 (November 1905-January 1906).

Barkin George, ed. *The Sardonic Humor of Ambrose Bierce*. New York: Dover Publications, 1963.

Bean, Walton, and Rawls, James J. *California: An Interpretive History*. 4th ed. New York: McGraw-Hill Book Co., 1983.

Beer, Thomas. *The Mauve Decade*. New York: Alfred A. Knopf, 1926.

Berkove, Lawrence I. "Ambrose Bierce's Concern with Mind and Man." Ph.D. dissertation, University of Pennsylvania, 1962.

_____. "The Man with the Burning Pen: Ambrose Bierce as Journalist." *Journal of Popular Culture*, 15 (1981): 34–40.

_____, ed. *Skepticism and Dissent: Selected Journalism of Ambrose Bierce from 1898 to 1901*. Ann Arbor: Delmas Books, 1980.

Bierce, Ambrose. *The Collected Works of Ambrose Bierce*. New York: The Neale Publishing Co., 1909–1912.

_____. *The Complete Short Stories of Ambrose Bierce*. Ernest Jerome Hopkins, ed. New York: Doubleday & Co., 1970.

_____. *The Devil's Dictionary*. New York: The Neale Publishing Co., 1911, Reprint, New York: Dover Publications, 1958.

_____. "If Reform Reformed." *Cosmopolitan,* 46 (December 1908): 1.

_____. *Write It Right*. New York: The Neale Publishing Co., 1909.

Bierce, Helen. "Ambrose Bierce at Home." *American Mercury*, 30 (December 1933): 453–458.

Bierce, Lucius Verus. *Travels in the Southland, 1822–1823: The Journal of Lucius Verus Bierce, with a Biographical Essay by George W. Knepper*. Columbus: Ohio State University Press, 1966.

Boller, Paul F. *Presidential Campaigns.* New York: Oxford University Press, 1984.

Brooks, Van Wyck. *Emerson and Others.* New York: E. P. Dutton & Co., 1927.

Bruce, John. *Gaudy Century: The Story of San Francisco's Hundred Years of Robust Journalism.* New York: Random House, 1948.

Chalmers, David Mark. *The Muckrake Years.* New York: D. Van Nostrand Co., 1974.

Cloud, Barbara. "Muckraking Gets Its Name." M.S. thesis, University of Oregon, 1967.

Coblenz, Edmond D., ed. *William Randolph Hearst: A Portrait in His Own Words.* New York: Simon and Schuster, 1952.

Daggett, Stuart. *Chapters on the History of the Southern Pacific.* New York: The Ronald Press Co., 1922.

Davidson, Cathy N. *Critical Essays on Ambrose Bierce.* Boston: G. K. Hall & Co., 1982.

_____. *The Experimental Fictions of Ambrose Bierce.* Lincoln: The University of Nebraska Press, 1984.

de Castro, Adolphe. *Portrait of Ambrose Bierce.* New York: The Century Co., 1929.

Dudley, Donald R. *A History of Cynicism.* London: Methuen & Co., 1937.

Evans, Cerinda W. *Collis Potter Huntington.* 2 vols. Newport News: The Mariners' Museum, 1954.

Fatout, Paul. *Ambrose Bierce: The Devil's Lexicographer.* Norman: University of Oklahoma Press, 1951.

_____. *Ambrose Bierce and the Black Hills.* Norman: University of Oklahoma Press, 1956.

Filler, Louis. *The Muckrakers.* University Park: Pennsylvania State University Press, 1976.

Flower, B. O. "Twenty-Five Years of Bribery and Corrupt Practises, or, the Railroads, the Lawmakers, the People." *Arena,* 26 (January 1904): 12–49.

Follett, Wilson. "America's Neglected Satirist." *The Dial,* 45 (18 July 1918): 49–52.

_____. "Ambrose, Son of Marcus Aurelius." *Atlantic Monthly,* 160 (July 1937) 32–42.

_____. "Bierce in His Brilliant Obscurity." *New York Times* (11 October 1936): 6:2.

Francendese, Janet M. "Ambrose Bierce as Journalist." Ph.D. dissertation, New York University, 1977.

Francke, Warren Theodore. "Investigative Exposure in the Nineteenth Century: The Journalistic Heritage of the Muckrakers." Ph.D. dissertation, University of Minnesota, 1974.

Frederick, Peter J. *Knights of the Golden Rule: The Intellectual as Christian Social Reformer in the 1890s.* Lexington: University Press of Kentucky, 1976.

Grassman, Curtis E. "Prologue to California Reform: The Democratic Impulse, 1886–1898." *Pacific Historical Review,* 42 (November 1973): 518–536.

Grattan, C. Hartley. *Bitter Bierce: A Mystery of American Letters.* New York: Doubleday & Co., 1929.

Grenander, Mary E. *Ambrose Bierce*. New York: Twayne Publishers, 1971.

Griffiths, David B. "Anti-Monopoly Movement in California: 1873–1898." *Southern California Quarterly*, 52 (June 1970): 93–112.

Hall, Oakley. *Ambrose Bierce and the Queen of Spades*. Berkeley: University of California Press, 1998.

Hart, Jerome A. *In Our Second Century*. San Francisco: The Pioneer Press, 1931.

Hofstadter, Richard. *The Age of Reform*. New York: Alfred A. Knopf, 1955.

Hoogenboom, Ari, and Hoogenboom, Olive, eds. *The Gilded Age*. Englewood Cliffs, N.J.: Prentice-Hall, 1967.

Hopkins, Ernest Jerome. "Bierce, Hearst, and the 'Rail-Rogue' Battle." Unpublished faculty research project, Arizona State University, 1967.

_____, ed. *The Ambrose Bierce Satanic Reader*. New York: Doubleday & Co., 1968.

Irwin, Will. *The American Newspaper*. Ames: The Iowa State University Press, 1969.

Johnson, Kenneth M. *The Sting of the Wasp: Political and Satirical Cartoons from the Truculent Early San Francisco Weekly*. San Francisco: Book Club of California, 1967.

Klein, Marcus. "San Francisco and Her Hateful Ambrose Bierce." *Hudson Review* (April 1954): 388–405.

Lavender, David. *The Great Persuader*. Garden City, N.Y.: Doubleday & Co., 1970.

Leach, Frank A. *Recollections of a Newspaperman*. San Francisco: Samuel Levinson, 1917.

Lewis, Oscar. *The Big Four*. New York: Alfred A. Knopf, 1969.

Martin, Albro. Railroads Triumphant. New York: Oxford University Press, 1992.

McKee, Irving. "The Background and Early Career of Hiram Warren Johnson, 1866–1910." *Pacific Historical Review*, 19 (February 1950): 17–30.

McWilliams, Carey. *Ambrose Bierce: A Biography*. New York: Albert & Charles Boni, 1929.

The Meditations of Marcus Aurelius Antoninus. Trans. John Jackson, with an introduction by Charles Bigg. London: Oxford at the Clarendon Press, 1906.

Mencken, H. L. *A Mencken Chrestomathy*. New York: Alfred A. Knopf, 1949.

Mercer, Lloyd J. *E. H. Harriman: Master Railroader*. Boston: Twayne Publishers, 1985.

Morris, Roy, Jr. *Ambrose Bierce: Alone in Bad Company*. New York: Crown Publishers, 1995.

Mott, Frank Luther. *A History of American Magazines*, 4 vols. Cambridge: Harvard University Press, 1957.

Mowry, George E. *The California Progressives*. Berkeley: University of California Press, 1951.

Neale, Walter. *Life of Ambrose Bierce*. New York: Walter Neale, 1929.

Noel, Joseph. *Footloose in Arcadia*. New York: Carrick & Evans, 1940.

Norris, Frank. *Novels and Essays*. New York: The Library of America, 1986.

Oates, Whitney J., ed. *The Stoic and Epicurean Philosophers: The Complete*

Extant Writings of Epicurus, Epictetus, Lucretius, and Marcus Aurelius. New York: Random House, 1940.

O'Connor, Richard. *Ambrose Bierce: A Biography.* Boston: Little, Brown & Co., 1967.

Older, Fremont. *Growing Up.* San Francisco: San Francisco Call-Bulletin, 1931.

————. *My Own Story.* San Francisco: The Call Publishing Co., 1919.

Older, Mrs. Fremont. *William Randolph Hearst: American.* New York: D. Appleton-Century Co., 1936.

Olin, Spencer C. Jr. *California's Prodigal Sons: Hiram Johnson and the Progressives, 1911–1917.* Berkeley: University of California Press, 1968.

Peterson, Theodore. *Magazines in the Twentieth Century.* Urbana: University of Illinois Press, 1964.

Pope, Bertha Clark, ed. *The Letters of Ambrose Bierce.* San Francisco: The Book Club of California, 1922.

Russell, Charles Edward. *Bare Hands and Stone Walls: Some Recollections of a Side-Line Reformer.* New York: Charles Scribner's Sons, 1933.

————. *Railroad Melons, Rates, and Wages: A Handbook of Railroad Information.* Chicago: Charles H. Kerr & Co., 1922.

Saunders, Richard. *Ambrose Bierce: The Making of a Misanthrope.* San Francisco: Chronicle Books, 1985.

Schlesinger, Arthur M., Jr. *The Cycles of American History.* Boston: Houghton Mifflin Co., 1986.

Sharp, Sarah Lee. "Social Criticism in California During the Gilded Age." Ph.D. dissertation, University of California, San Diego, 1979.

Smith, Edwin W. *The Life and Times of Daniel Lindley: 1801–1880.* London: The Epworth Press, 1949.

Sterling, George. "The Shadow Maker." *American Mercury,* 6 (September 1925) 10–19.

Swanberg, W. A. *Citizen Hearst.* New York: Charles Scribner's Sons, 1961.

————. *Whitney Father, Whitney Heiress.* New York: Charles Scribner's Sons, 1980.

Takaki, Ronald. *Iron Cages: Race and Culture in Nineteenth-Century America.* New York: Alfred A. Knopf, 1979.

Tarbell, Ida. *All in the Day's Work.* Boston: G. K. Hall & Co., 1985.

Tebbel, John, and Zuckerman, Mary Ellen. *The Magazine in America: 1741–1990.* New York: Oxford University Press, 1991.

Walker, Franklin. *Ambrose Bierce: The Wickedest Man in San Francisco.* San Francisco: The Colt Press, 1941.

Walters, Ronald G. *American Reformers: 1815–1860.* New York: Hill & Wang, 1978.

Ward, James A. *Railroads and the Character of America, 1820–1887.* Knoxville: University of Tennessee Press, 1986.

West, George P. "Hearst: A Psychological Note." *American Mercury,* 21 (November 1930) 298–308.

Wiggins, Robert A. *Ambrose Bierce.* Minneapolis: University of Minnesota Press, 1964.

Winkler, John K. *William Randolph Hearst: A New Appraisal*. New York: Hastings House, 1955.
Young, John P. *Journalism in California*. San Francisco: Chronicle Publishing Co., 1915.

PERIODICALS

The Argonaut, 25 March 1877–17 May 1879.
The Wasp, 27 May 1881–11 September 1886.
The San Francisco Examiner, 4 July 1887–1 October 1901.
Cosmopolitan, 1905–1909.

UNPUBLISHED LETTERS AND PAPERS

Bierce collection, the Green Library, Stanford University, Palo Alto, California.
The Collis P. Huntington Papers, microfilm edition.

Index

About the Author

DANIEL LINDLEY is an editor and journalist who has written for numerous magazines and newspapers.

ISBN 0-275-96696-8

90000>

EAN

9 780275 966966

HARDCOVER BAR CODE